HERE'S
SAVANNAH

*A Journey through
Historic Savannah & Environs*

Susan H. Albu
&
Elizabeth Arndt

HERE'S SAVANNAH
A Journey through
Historic Savannah & Environs

Copyright © 1994
A & A Enterprises

———

ISBN 0-9640597-1-1

Photography by Elizabeth Arndt

Printed in the United States of America
Atlantic Printing Company
Savannah, Georgia

TABLE OF CONTENTS

I

First Came the Indians

For thousands of years before the coming of the Europeans, the Southeast was inhabited by Indians, who may have reached the Georgia coast as early as 15,000 years ago. The culture of these earliest Indians was quite unlike our concept of Indian life. At this time they had no agriculture, pottery, or bows and arrows, just spears and a few small tools whose use is mostly archaeological guesswork. Through the next several millennia cultural development was uneven. Coastal Georgia has some of the earliest pottery in North America, yet was one of the latest areas to acquire maize or corn agriculture.

Some of the earliest Indian sites in the Savannah area, dating from as far back as 3,000 B.C. are the famed "shell middens". These are just huge piles of oyster shell discarded by the Indians, sort of prehistoric garbage dumps. Sometimes animal and fish bones and fragments of pottery and stone tools are also found among the shells. The middens can be irregular heaps, or crescent or ring-shaped. The shell rings have provoked the greatest interest. Some are quite large, such as a ring on Sapelo Island which is 300' across and 8' tall in places. The center of the ring is usually just bare sandy soil, leading early archaeologists to speculate that the rings were ceremonial structures, possibly the oldest in the Americas. A less romantic explanation may be that they were village sites surrounded by a circular palisade, and oyster shells and other refuse were piled up outside the palisade.

Shell rings can be found in the Savannah area along the eastern shorelines of Wilmington Island (at least two) and Skidaway Island (at least three). In addition to the rings there are dozens of shell middens in the Savannah area, including out in the salt marshes. Here they take on the appearance of small desert islands lost in a sea of marsh grass, with palmettoes, cedars and other hardy plants growing in the soil held in place by the shells. Not all of these small marsh islands, known

5

locally as "hammocks" are archaeological sites, but many are. Often shell midden sites continued in use by the Indians until the coming of the Europeans, as fish and shellfish remained an important part of the Indian diet.

Around 1,500 B.C. these sites begin to yield some of the oldest pottery in North America. Clay used to make this pottery seems to have been mixed with some kind of plant material, probably Spanish moss or palmetto fiber before firing to make it stronger. It is often referred to as fiber-tempered pottery, and has been found in many Southeastern sites far inland from the coast, as well as in the Caribbean and along the northern coast of South America.

By the time of Christ, the bow and arrow came into use, greatly increasing the efficiency of the hunter or warrior, pottery became much more refined, and agriculture had its beginnings. One of the earliest

Crescent Shaped Shell Mound, Skidaway Island

crops was tobacco, known from the many pipes found in archaeological sites. By 900 A.D. corn began to be grown as a staple crop. Burial mounds erected for the interment of chiefs and other important people became common. A famous burial mound known as the Indian King's Tomb was located near the intersection of Montgomery Crossroads and Hodgson Memorial Drive, next to Bartlett Middle School.

6

Excavated during the 1920's, it contained the burials of more than 40 individuals and quantities of grave goods, such as pottery, weapons and beads. It was destroyed as a nuisance in 1950.

Savannah's most famous Indian site was probably the Irene Mound, once located at the juncture of Pipemaker's Canal and the Savannah River near Garden City. It was excavated during the Depression from 1937-39, under the direction of the Works Progress Administration. Dating from around 1200-1550 A.D. the Irene Mound was discovered to be a ceremonial complex which included a platform mound with the remains of a temple, a burial mound, council house, several smaller mounds and a village site. It was similar to other ceremonial centers in Georgia, such as the Etowah, Ocmulgee and Kolomoki Mounds, only smaller, the tallest mound in the complex being only 15 feet high! It has been the only such site ever found on the Georgia coast. Unfortunately, it was completely leveled during excavation because of the anticipated industrial use of the area. The site is now covered by a Ports Authority warehouse.

Culturally, all the ceremonial centers are associated with the "Southern Cult", which included maize or corn agriculture, and elaborate religious rituals and art work, thought to have been derived from the Mayan and Aztec civilizations of Mexico. Southern Cult sites range from Oklahoma to the Atlantic coast, with the majority being concentrated in the lower Mississippi River valley. By the time Europeans began to explore the Southeast, the Indian chiefdoms of the Savannah area seem to have been in a decline. Early Spanish accounts from the 1500's describe the Savannah River valley as practically uninhabited, a sort of buffer zone between warring tribes to the north and to the south.

In 1562-3 Jean Ribaut established a short-lived French outpost named Charlesfort on Parris Island, near Beaufort, South Carolina. Only three years later in 1565, on the same island, Spain planted the colony of Santa Elena, which became the capital of Spanish Florida. It was abandoned 22 years later as undefensible after Sir Francis Drake's attack on St. Augustine in the same year. In spite of this setback, Spanish missions along the Georgia coast at St. Catherine's Island and other places flourished for another hundred years until the 1680's when again threatened by English attacks. At this time missionaries and christianized Indians fled from the Georgia missions to St. Augustine, then the capital of Florida. Meanwhile, the English continued to push southward from Virginia, and in 1629 King Charles I of England claimed the Carolinas for England. Permanent English settlement at Charleston in 1670, and at Beaufort in 1711 served to open up the area southward to further English colonization. This land eventually came to be known as Georgia.

Irene Period Pottery with Paddle Stamp

II

The Grand Plan

The Colony of Georgia was founded by James Edward Oglethorpe. He was born in London on December 22, 1696, the seventh of nine children of Theophilus and Eleanor Wall Oglethorpe. After attending Eton and Corpus Christi College, Oxford, he entered the military service. In 1722 he was elected to Parliament, a seat he would hold until 1755. Oglethorpe would live in Georgia and guide the fledgling colony for slightly more than ten years of his life but his concern about its progress would last all his years. He left Georgia for the last time on July 22, 1743. After returning to England, he married Elizabeth Wright in 1745. There were no children born to their union. Oglethorpe died in 1785 and was buried in a simple grave in Cranham.

His service in Parliament and the military developed Oglethorpe's awareness of social problems in England. In 1728, his good friend, Robert Castell published a book, *Villas of the Ancients*. It was not a financial success and Castell landed in debtors' prison. Before Oglethorpe could obtain his friend's release, Castell contracted smallpox and died. This episode had a deep and lasting effect on Oglethorpe. As a member of Parliament, he formed a committee to study the deplorable jail conditions and some improvements were made. Through this process, Oglethorpe and the other committee members learned of otherwise good men who had fallen into debt and been jailed as was the custom. The jail committee members wanted to do more and felt that such men should have more options. From that committee, many of the Trustees of Georgia were chosen.

For many years there had been talk in England about forming another colony and Oglethorpe and the jail committee members considered such a plan a fine outlet for the debtors. The original Georgia Charter names the desperately poor as proper colonists, persons who were "reduced to great necessity, insomuch that by their labor they are not able to provide a maintenance for themselves and families". These guidelines were carefully followed as no one was to leave who could be a productive citizen in England. Exactly how many of the early

REASONS

FOR ESTABLISHING THE

COLONY OF GEORGIA,

WITH REGARD TO THE

TRADE OF GREAT BRITAIN,

THE

Increase of our People, and the Employment and Support it will afford to great Numbers of our own Poor, as well foreign persecuted Protestants.

With some Account of the Country, and the design of the Trustees.

———

Hoc Natura præscribit, ut homo homini, quicunque sit, ob eam ipsam Causam tamen, quod is homo sit, consultum velit.
                                                                    CICERO DE OFFICIIS, LIB. III.

———

LONDON:
1733.

1 0

colonists were truly debtors has been the topic of much historical research. The current belief is that no more than one third of the colonists were actually debtors but nearly all were desperately poor.

A few colonists paid their own passage and expenses. Some settlers were economic refugees who were indentured servants bound to work out their passage, usually five to seven years. Other colonists came to Georgia after fleeing religious oppression. Such groups included the Jews who came in 1733 after escaping the Spanish Inquisition, the Salzburgers, Moravians, and many other groups from Middle Europe.

England, a country of merchants, had some very materialistic reasons for wanting Georgia to be established. The colony would remove persons who were unable to support themselves and they might even become taxpayers in the colony. England wanted a buffer to protect prosperous South Carolina from the Spaniards in Florida who kept creeping up the coast. A colony that could produce raw materials such as silk, grapes, hemp, and indigo for export to the manufacturers in England then purchase the finished products to be shipped back to Georgia seemed a fine plan. All of this and they also had the moral satisfaction of a colony where the poor and religiously oppressed could go and begin a new life.

The Original Seal of Georgia
"Not For Themselves But Others"

These reasons, with broad appeal, allowed the Trustees of Georgia to proceed with their plans for the colony. To ensure the King's interest and help, they named the colony for King George II. The original 21 Trustees were high minded men who wanted the Georgia colony to be different, one where each man had an equal chance. The Trustees adopted as their motto the Latin Phrase, "Non Sibi Sed Aliis" which translated means, "Not for themselves but others". The seal featured mulberries and silkworms, an indication of the importance they placed on the colony's anticipated ability to produce silk. Unlike other colonies, the Trustees did not want to reap huge profits so they said that no Trustee could own Georgia land. This included Oglethorpe who never owned any land in Georgia. They could have no salary. Gradually the number of Trustees increased to 72, the later Trustees paying for the honor, another way to raise badly needed funds to support the venture. The rules they imposed on themselves were strict as were the following prohibitions which they imposed upon the colonists:

> Prohibition I: There was to be no rum, brandy or spirits in Georgia as the Trustees felt it would be bad for the colonists. This led to much smuggling and many stills. Wine, beer and ale were permitted.

> Prohibition II: There were to be no lawyers in the colony. Oglethorpe, possibly due to his experiences with the English jails, felt that each man should speak for himself or get a friend to act in his behalf.

> Prohibition III: There were to be no black slaves or Negroes in Georgia. Georgia was the only free colony. Slaves were borrowed from South Carolina to help clear the land and from the beginning, the colonists petitioned to have slaves. In 1751 this was repealed and slavery was permitted.

> Prohibition IV: All were to have freedom of religion except Papists (Catholics). It was felt their allegiance might be to the Catholics in the Spanish colony in Florida and thus endanger the colony.

They considered a fifth prohibition which would have barred gold or silver in clothing or furniture but all the colonists were so terribly poor, it was deemed unnecessary. The theories, the rules and the charter were done. The colonists, led by Oglethorpe were about to depart.

III

Here They Come

The first 114 settlers, led by Oglethorpe, sailed from England on September 11, 1732 on the Ship *Anne*. Despite the high rate of illiteracy among the passengers, the ship was loaded with hundreds of prayerbooks and temperance tracts. Oglethorpe alone went ashore at their first stop, Charleston, S.C. The *Anne* then proceeded to Beaufort where all disembarked. Oglethorpe and a small party advanced to select a site for the colony. Coming up the Savannah River, Oglethorpe chose the site and as these excerpts from the *Colonial Records of Georgia* report, he wrote to his fellow Trustees:

> *"I chose the Situation for the Town upon high Ground. Forty Feet perpendicular above High-water mark; the Soil dry and sandy, the Water of the River fresh; Springs coming out from the sides of the hills.... it is sheltered from the Western and Southern Winds by vast Woods of Pine trees, many of which are a Hundred, and few under Seventy Feet High....The last and fullest Conviction of the Healthfulness of the Place was, that an Indian Nation, who knew the nature of this country, chose it for their Situation."*

Tomochichi, chief or Mico of the Yamacraw Indians, and his small band of about 45 received Oglethorpe and his party. The Yamacraw were part of the Lower Creek Indians and had separated from the others after the Yemasee Wars in South Carolina. They had been living on the bluff since 1728. Relations between Oglethorpe and Tomochichi were good from the beginning and strengthened by good treaties, they remained so. On May 13, 1733, a Treaty of Friendship was signed which agreed that the English could settle any land but Ossabaw, Sapelo, and St. Catherine's Islands which were to remain Indian land forever. The Treaty also established a trade and value schedule and bound the Indians to support the English cause against the Spanish or French.

Mary Musgrove, Princess Cousaponakeesa, was an Indian Princess whose father was a white man who arranged for her education in Charleston. She married John Musgrove, another half-breed and together, they had established a trading post in the Savannah area. By this time the Indians had become accustomed to dealing with whites and were very much involved in trade in furs and deerskins. These

Mico of the Yamacraw
Tomochichi and His Nephew Toonahowi

Indians were referred to as "Trader's Indians". The Musgroves would be of great value to Oglethorpe as they acted as arbiters and interpreters as well as a source of much needed supplies. Through the years Mary

Musgrove would marry three times. Her last husband was Rev. Thomas Bosomworth, an aggressive man who pushed her to take her fight for the Indian lands, Ossabaw, Sapelo and St. Catherine's to the British Courts. She ultimately won her claim and in 1750, she was granted St. Catherine's Island making her the largest landowner in Georgia at that time.

The site having been selected, Oglethorpe led his band of settlers up the Savannah River to their new home on the 40 foot bluff. They landed on February 1, 1733 but when the change to the Gregorian calendar was made, the date became February 12, 1733. Soon the colony's first child, Georgia Close, was born to Henry and Hannah Close on March 17, 1733. Although he had no legislated powers, Oglethorpe was referred to by the colonists as 'Father Oglethorpe' and he was without question, their leader.

Shortly after the English came, the Indians would move to a spot about four miles upriver to what we know as the Irene Mound Site. A tract of land several square miles in size surrounding the Irene Mound was reserved for the use of the Indians. It was surveyed and carefully delineated with posts and trees with red and white markings on them. Tomochichi would even build a house in the English style. The Musgroves relocated their trading post, the Cowpen, to the Indian land, choosing a spot on the Savannah River near the present Savannah Sugar Refinery. The Indians did not camp on the Irene Mound Site itself as they considered it haunted, possibly from the number of skeletal remains which kept eroding from the burial mound! In 1736 less superstitious Anglican and Moravian missionaries erected an Indian Mission on the mound which lasted only three years until 1739 when Tomochichi died. Shortly after his death, the Indians abandoned their village, New Yamacraw, and left Savannah never to return.

IV

Getting Settled

The city plan for Savannah which Oglethorpe brought with him in 1733 has remained world famous to the present time. The origin of the plan for the squares as laid out remains unknown although much study has produced many possible sources. Perhaps it was Oglethorpe's concept of English villages and commons that he expanded to the urban plan that eventually led to 24 squares, 22 of which have been retained.

The first square laid out in 1733, was Johnson Square. Public ovens, a well, and an area for common defense were part of the square. The next squares also laid out the first year were Ellis, Reynolds, and Wright Squares (then Percival Square). The land was allocated to the settlers according to their status. The settler who came at his own expense and brought four white male indentured servants received the largest allocation of land, 500 acres. The charity colonist who did not pay his own passage, received 50 acres. Many servants would serve five to seven years indenture then receive a cow, a sow, and 50 acres of land.

The land was granted with a city lot, called a tything lot, which measured 60 x 90 feet; a five acre garden plot just outside the city; a 44 acre farm lot beyond the garden lots and if granted 500 acres, the balance would be at a distance from the settlement. In the beginning the colonists lived in tents. The first houses in the town were cottage like structures that were 24' wide, 18' deep, and 8' high. These structures may have been prefabricated in Charleston to help get the settlers under roof quickly. The colonists, many city folk, had few skills to develop the community. Slaves were borrowed from South Carolina and were used to clear the land and erect the first buildings. Sticking to the prohibition against slavery, Oglethorpe had them returned as soon as possible to South Carolina. The hardships of life in the colony coupled with the work the colonists saw the slaves complete soon started the drive for slavery in the colony. The Trustees held out until 1751 when slavery was allowed.

The Trustees, naturally anxious to learn about their venture, had Peter Gordon draw them a map entitled "A View of Savannah as it

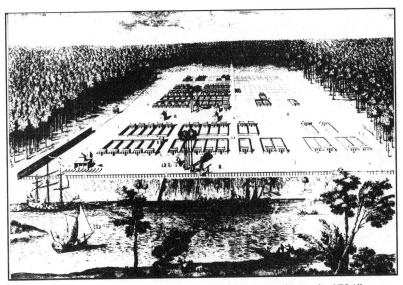

"A View of Savannah as it stood the 29th of March, 1734"

stood the 29th of March, 1734". It shows the orderly pattern of the little houses laid out around the first squares and the entire area surrounded by dense pine forests.

A priority in the colony was the growing of mulberry trees which in turn would make silk production possible. To this end, Oglethorpe set aside ten acres down the bluff for the purpose of establishing an experimental garden, the first one in any American colony. The site, called Trustee's Garden, was in the area of the present Pirate's House Restaurant. Emphasis was on making silk production possible. So keen were the English on this venture that Paul Amatis, an Italian silkmaker, came with them to oversee the effort. One of the first large buildings was the Filature House, built on Reynolds Square for the reeling of silk. Despite their best efforts, silk worms were not happy in Georgia and the most silk produced was eight pounds sent to Queen Charlotte who made it into a dress which she wore on her birthday. The old Filature House, after the silk effort failed, was the first public meeting house and served as an early theater before it was destroyed by fire in 1849.

Other plants, brought from England, and some obtained in the Caribbean were nurtured in the garden then the seedlings were given to the colonists. The garden did rather well until some of Savannah's infrequent frosts hit the tropical garden. By 1755 there was little left of the original garden so it was abandoned and houses were built on the site.

In 1734 Oglethorpe took Tomochichi, his wife Senauki, his nephew Toonahowi and a few other Indians to England to meet the King. John Musgrove accompanied them as interpreter. Indians were very fascinating to the Englishmen of this period and Georgia's Indians were a great sensation. Tomochichi was the subject of several paintings. A copper plate made from a Verelst painting survives and may be seen at the Savannah History Museum. Tomochichi seemed to have had great affection for Oglethorpe and the colonists. He moved his home to Pipemaker's Creek and built a house in the English style. He asked to be buried among the English in Savannah and this was done. Tomochichi died, reportedly at age 97, in 1739. He was buried in the center of Percival Square (now Wright Square) and a crude marker was erected which was destroyed in 1884 when the monument to William Washington Gordon was erected on that spot. Later, a boulder was placed on the southeast corner of the square with a plaque honoring the Mico of the Yamacraw.

Because of the concern for their safety, Oglethorpe began to establish outposts and fortifications surrounding the city thus beginning the development of the rest of the area.

V

Out In The Boondocks

Oglethorpe brought with him not only a plan for the city of Savannah, but a plan for the entire colony of Georgia. It is not surprising that the Trustees entrusted the founding of the colony to a military man, Oglethorpe, since one of the prime reasons for establishing it was military. The colony was intended to provide a buffer between the wealthy English colony of South Carolina, and the Spanish in Florida. Historians have noted that the town plan of Savannah with its squares and broad avenues was well suited for military defense. The squares could be used to assemble and drill troops, and the avenues to move them around readily from one fortification to another.

As more and more people arrived in the colony, Oglethorpe began to assign them to what he referred to as "out-villages", giving each settler a house lot and a 50-acre tract of land. These settlements were little more than small fortified outposts. Each had a blockhouse and cannon, and the settlers were expected to stand a 24 hour watch as well as drill regularly. A "tythingman" was assigned as the peace officer to each village, who saw to the settlers' military duties. The English settlers complained loudly about such extra responsibilities, but the German and Swiss accepted them without murmur as their countries had universal military service.

Oglethorpe managed well the mixture of various groups of economic and religious refugees that made up the early citizenry of Georgia. Most of the early villages he created had about a dozen households of people of similar origin or language. French speakers, for example, were assigned to the village of Highgate. (These were probably French Swiss.) German speakers went to another village, Hampstead, which they promptly christened Heimstatt, not knowing of the London suburb for which the village was named.

Only the German and Swiss indentured servants were scattered among settlers in the English areas, such as Skidaway Island, Thunderbolt, Beaulieu Plantation, or Savannah itself. In addition to indentured servants, charity colonists and soldiers, the colony had an elite group of English settlers who were able to pay their own way and bring their own indentured servants. These individuals were eligible for the 500-acre grants, the largest tract of land that could be owned by one person or organization under the rules of the Trusteeship. Included among them were Thomas Causton with his grant, "Ockstead", Noble Jones with "Wormsloe", Thomas Parker and Henry Fallowfield of the Isle of Hope area, William Stephens with "Beaulieu", Roger Lacey in the Thunderbolt area, and various others. Religious or charitable organizations also received grants. Bethesda Orphanage received a 500-acre grant, which it still owns. The Anglican church, Christ Church, received glebe land for its support, as did the original White Bluff Meeting House.

Most of the outposts along navigable waterways were settled by

Wormsloe Gate

English colonists. These included Tybee Island, where the settlers built and maintained the first lighthouse erected in 1736, and places along the Inland Passage, forerunner to today's Intracoastal Waterway, which ran southward along the coast. Here were established Thunderbolt and Skidaway in 1734 and Jones's Fort on Wormsloe in 1736. West of Savannah, along the Ogeechee River were two forts, First Fort and Fort Argyle, which were manned intermittently by Scottish soldiers, along with some Germans and Swiss. A group of Scots also settled Joseph's Town north of Savannah on the Savannah River.

Located about 25 miles north of Savannah was the town of Ebenezer and the settlement area of the Salzburgers, Lutheran refugees from Germany and Austria. Old Ebenezer was established in 1734, under the leadership of pastors Johann Boltzius and Israel Gronau. It was moved within a few months to its present site at the juncture of Ebenezer Creek and the Savannah River. The town was laid out in a plan similar to Savannah with squares and town lots, though much simpler. Several boat loads, or what are known as "transports" of German Lutherans, arrived within the next few years.

Other German and Swiss colonists, of the Calvinist German or Swiss Reformed Church arrived and were given the villages of Hampstead and Highgate, located about four miles directly south of Savannah, about where the northern boundary of Hunter Air Field is now. Why many of these villages and forts were spaced about four miles apart is somewhat of a mystery, although it probably has some military significance. The last of these settlements were created in 1742 when a large number of German and Swiss indentured servants finished their term of indenture and asked for the land they had been promised. Most had arrived in 1735-36 and had finished their five to seven year term of indenture. Oglethorpe created two new villages for them, Vernonburg for the Germans and Acton for the Swiss. Vernonburg was located about where present day Vernonburg is, and Acton was probably a mile or two to the northeast. It is believed that Hayner's Creek, which flows under the Montgomery Crossroads bridge near Waters Avenue, was named after one of Acton's Swiss settlers, Nicholas Hanner.

The two towns shared a church with a German-speaking pastor named Johann Joachim Zubly. Eventually the congregation became known as the White Bluff Meeting House. Today it is the White Bluff Presbyterian Church, now housed a modern building. Behind it is a old graveyard where some of the descendants of the area's original settlers have been laid to rest. Since most of these settlers were members of the German and Swiss Reformed Church and followers of Calvin, it was appropriate to become Presbyterian, because Presbyterianism is also based upon Calvinist doctrine.

All four villages were located on the Vernonburg Road, which closely corresponds to present White Bluff Road. (During the 19th century Vernonburg was known as White Bluff.) The Vernonburg Road began at the end of Bull Street then near Oglethorpe Avenue. Hampstead was probably located along the road about four miles from Savannah, and Vernonburg about eight. Later, a German settler, Michael Burkehalter was to establish a 500 acre farm southwest of Vernonburg on what became known as Dutchtown Road, named for Burkehalter and other German settlers who lived there. Unlike the Salzburgers who retained much of their cultural identity longer, the Germans and Swiss in the Savannah area were rapidly assimilated into the British population.

Even earlier than White Bluff Road was the Bethesda Road, made to accommodate travel to the eastern part of the county. Here much transportation was by water, rather than land because all of the settlements were on the Inland Passage. Bethesda Road left the city on the eastern side, about where Wheaton Street runs today, probably connecting to present Skidaway Road. Roads branched off to the east leading to Thomas Causton's Ockstead and Thunderbolt. At about present day Sandfly, a road to Skidaway Island forked off through Wormsloe property across a shallow tidal river to an island, then across another tidal creek to Skidaway Island proper. Eventually two bridges were built here. From present day Sandfly the Bethesda Road then turned west and continued several miles to end at the Bethesda Orphanage.

The Bethesda Road allowed contact between all the settlements and villages along the Inland Passage, from Causton Bluff to Skidaway Island, and westward to Bethesda itself, and the adjoining plantation of Beaulieu, home of William Stephens, President of the Georgia after the departure of Oglethorpe in 1743. Eventually a road connecting Bethesda and Acton, following the general course of Waters Avenue and Montgomery Crossroads, joined Vernonburg and Bethesda Roads.

Most communication to the settlements south of Savannah was by boat on the Inland Passage, but there was a route later called the Darien Road, said to have been an old Indian path, which connected Savannah to the town of Darien. On the outskirts of Savannah it came to be called the Ogeechee Road because it led to a crossing of the Ogeechee River near Fort Argyle. Later, this road was sometimes referred to as the Great Ogeechee Plank Road, because of the use of wooden planks as a road bed, especially in marshy areas. Bethesda and Vernonburg Roads, which were close to salt water were paved with shells.

Running northwest from the city of Savannah paralleling the Savannah River was the Augusta Road, along which were a similar grouping of settlements. At four miles from Savannah was New Yamacraw and the Indian Land, at eight miles the settlement of Joseph's Town, and at twelve miles the village of Abercorn. Beyond was the large tract of land assigned to the Salzburgers. About 125 miles north of Savannah Oglethorpe founded the town of Augusta in 1737. Like Savannah it began with an already existing trading post and nearby Indian village.

More threatening than the French and Indians, from which the settlement at Augusta was supposed to defend the colony, were the Spanish, who actually claimed the land that had been newly christened Georgia. Oglethorpe had discussed English claims to land north of the Altamaha River with a Spanish representative in a meeting on St. Simons Island. Unfortunately, the Spaniard who had agreed to consider the claim was recalled to Spain and executed as a traitor! In 1736 Oglethorpe had founded Fort Frederica, building both the town and fort on the north end of St. Simons Island. In 1742 the Spaniards landed on St. Simons, attacked Oglethorpe's forces and were defeated in the Battle of Bloody Marsh. Never again did the Spanish pose a threat to the colony of Georgia. Oglethorpe left the colony in 1743, newly promoted to General, confident that the danger was past.

For ten years after his departure, the Trustees continued their stewardship. Many of the villages, such as the one on Skidaway Island had been abandoned by 1740, and others even earlier. Most of the Englishmen were city dwellers who had no knowledge of farming, so they fared poorly. Even the most enterprising ones gave up and moved to Savannah or to other colonies. The letters of these early settlers give a glimpse of life in the "out-villages". For example Thomas Mouse of Skidaway Island seems to have tried everything possible to hang on, including running a tavern and store with his wife and four daughters. Tavern-keeping had its high and low points. The Mouse's tavern entertained John Wesley on several occasions when he came to conduct services for the residents of Skidaway Island. The low point came when Thomas Causton, Savannah's bailiff, threatened to close the tavern down for serving liquor to Indians, which was against the law.

Most settlers complained of the restriction on the size of their holdings, which were limited to 50 acres, and the prohibition of slavery. The economic downturn in Savannah which began when Trustee funds began to be diverted for the establishment of Fort Frederica in 1736, continued. As the colony reached a crisis point, the Trustees reluctantly began to change the rules. Most important was the end of the prohibition of slavery effective January 1, 1751. Finally in 1752, a year before the charter was to end, the Trustees turned over the colony to the Crown.

From then on, Georgia developed a plantation economy similar to South Carolina's. Oglethorpe's planned colony was all but erased. Of the early land grants only Wormsloe and Bethesda retained their acreage, and only Wormsloe has a structure dating from the Trusteeship period. This is the ruins of Noble Jones's fortified dwelling built 1736-39, an unusual building constructed of tabby, a type of cement made of oyster shell. The 18" thick walls surrounding the house would seem to be meant to withstand Spanish cannon rather than Indian arrows! The fort was once meant to challenge Spanish invaders coming up the Inland Passage to Savannah, but the recent dredging of a new channel close to Skidaway Island dried up the original channel to a mere trickle seen only at high tide. The descendants of Noble Jones kept the property remarkably intact and in 1974 much of the site was donated to the State of Georgia as a park.

A few villages like Vernonburg and Thunderbolt and plantations such as Beaulieu persisted as place names. The town of Vernonburg was sold by the congregation of the White Bluff Meeting House in 1799 and became part of a plantation. The later settlement of the Vernonburg area, then known as White Bluff, grew up in the 1840's along the waterfront as a summer resort, not at the site of the colonial town. In fact in the colonial plan, it appeared that the waterfront area was to be reserved for warehouses and docks, much like Savannah's River Street.

In the 1750's deeds and tax records show small holdings, such as the original settlers' 50-acre lots becoming absorbed into larger farms and plantations. Places that were formerly not usable as farm land, such as the river swamps were transformed into rice fields with the use of slave labor. Aerial photographs of the Savannah, Little Ogeechee and Ogeechee River basins clearly show the squared off rice fields and canals in the swamps. Much of the land on the islands was used for dry rice culture and the growing of indigo. A wide variety of food crops were grown in addition to these cash crops. Some non-commercial experimentation was done with growing sea island cotton, and the first cotton crop in Georgia is said to have been raised by John Earle on Skidaway Island in 1767.

One of the few structures which has survived from this period is Wild Heron, a plantation house on the Little Ogeechee River which was once located on a rice plantation. The land was granted in 1747 to David Cutler Braddock, and it is assumed he built the house between 1752-56 because he borrowed large sums of money during that period. In 1756 the property was bought by Francis Harris whose wife may have named the plantation after her ancestral home in England. The plantation house is believed to be the oldest surviving building in Georgia. A plantation tract which has survived from this period is that of Lebanon Plantation on Ogeechee Road. It was granted in 1756 to James Deveaux. Many other plantations in the Savannah area which became important in the antebellum period were begun at this time. Particularly famous were the wealthy rice plantations along the Savannah River, extending from Causton's Bluff and Deptford in the south to Mulberry Grove and Rice Hope in the north. Rice was planted up to the city limits until 1819, when yellow fever measures took land around the city out of cultivation.

Places that had been abandoned earlier, such as Skidaway Island, were resettled. "New Village" was established near the southern end of the island, far from "Old Village" located on present Skidaway Institute of Oceanography land. Other islands were resettled or granted such as Wilmington, Whitemarsh, Wassaw, Dutch and Ossabaw. Dutch Island, as its name suggests, was owned at different times by several German families, the Herbs, Radicks and Danzlers. Ossabaw Island was

Wild Heron Plantation

acquired in 1760 by Mary Musgrove who won Ossabaw along with St. Catherine's and Sapelo in a lawsuit against the Colony of Georgia. Unfortunately, Ossabaw and Sapelo soon were confiscated for debts she owed to the Crown and granted to plantation owners. Ossabaw eventually came into possession of the Morel family originally of Highgate, who also owned Beaulieu Plantation in the latter part of the colonial period. At Beaulieu John Morel operated a shipyard for a short time, in a small inlet, now known as Shipyard Creek, right off the Inland Passage.

Most of the shipbuilding and repair activity in the Savannah area actually took place in the Savannah and Hutchinson Island wharf areas, near present River Street. With the increased ship traffic, particularly the importation of slaves, a Lazaretto or quarantine station was built at

Tybee Island. The 1742 Tybee lighthouse structure, which Oglethorpe proudly described as "much the best building of that kind in America", was repaired in the 1770s, and eventually rebuilt further inland in 1791.

View of "Tiby" Lighthouse, 1764

Let Us Pray

The Georgia Trustees proclaimed that there would be freedom of religion in their colony except for Papists (Catholics) whom they felt might have overwhelming loyalties to the Catholics of Spanish Florida and thus be a threat to the colony. This freedom of religion would make Savannah an attractive haven to many religiously oppressed people.

Christ Episcopal Church, Johnson Square

The dominant religion of the Georgia Trustees and the first colonists was Anglican. One of the first acts of Oglethorpe as he laid out Johnson Square was to designate the eastern Trust Lot for the erection of the Anglican church. Trust Lots were given for government buildings, churches or other facilities for public use. The first Anglican minister, Rev. Henry Herbet, came on the *Anne* with Ogle-thorpe. He died on the return voyage. Next came Rev. Samuel Quincy of the famous New England family. He was unpopular and stayed only a brief time. The Society for the Propagation of the Gospel provided these ministers as they did for outposts everywhere. The Society then sent the brothers John and Charles Wesley who arrived in 1736.

Charles Wesley proceeded to Ft. Frederica south of Savannah where he was secretary to Oglethorpe. His stay was short and he soon returned to England. Rev. John Wesley was the Anglican pastor in Savannah and his residence was on the southwest Trust Lot on Reynolds Square. He had a broad approach to religion and worked closely with the Moravian and Jewish communities. While in Savannah he established the world's first Sunday School in 1736. His ministry became troubled because of his affection for a young lady named Sophia Hopkey. There are various versions of this story but essentially the young Wesley was much taken by Miss Hopkey but she did not return his affection as she loved another. She decided to marry William Williamson and Wesley refused to announce their bans of marriage. She was married in South Carolina and upon return, Wesley refused to give her communion. This public insult caused her new husband to sue Wesley for defamation of character. Wesley saw it as a church matter over which civil courts had no jurisdiction but the litigation proceeded and it greatly interfered with his ministry. Wesley left Savannah after one year and nine months and returned to England where he and his brother Charles would found the Methodist Church.

The earliest Anglican services were held in various places including Oglethorpe's tent. As early as 1739 tons of flintstones, iron from Russia and other building materials began arriving for the erection of the Anglican Church. It would be the colony's fourth pastor, Rev. George Whitefield, who actually laid the foundation of the church in 1740. It was dedicated in 1750 and burned in the fire of 1796. A second church was destroyed by a hurricane and rebuilt by 1815. In 1838 it was demolished and the present building begun. That church burned in 1897 but some of the walls and the foundation were saved and the rebuilt church is the present Christ Church on Johnson Square still on the original site designated by Oglethorpe.

Rev. Whitefield was an enormously popular preacher of international fame who used his skills to raise funds for philanthropic projects. He knew the brothers Wesley in England and from them learned of the need for an orphanage for the children in the new colony. He petitioned the Georgia Trustees and was granted 500 acres to establish an orphanage on the site that to this day has remained Bethesda Orphanage. The road to Bethesda was the first road of any length in Georgia. Bethesda, established in 1740, is said to be the oldest orphanage in the United States in continual operation. The original Bethesda site contained a central building in the raised cottage style with a high pitched roof and a porch to catch the breezes. Surrounding this were small cottages for the children. The old buildings have long

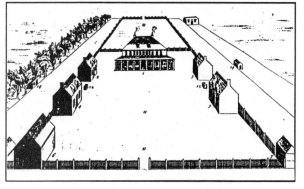

Bethesda Orphanage, c. 1740

ago disappeared and today the oldest building dates to 1883. There is a small museum about life at Bethesda which is open to the public. In 1925 a small c h a p e l , dedicated to the memory of Rev. Whitefield was completed. It is said to resemble Whitefield's chapel in England and was built by the National Society of Colonial Dames in America in the State of Georgia. The Bethesda Gate was completed in 1940 with the help of the Bethesda boys and dedicated on the 200th anniversary of the institution.

Just five months after Oglethorpe and the first colonists arrived, a group of 42 Jewish people arrived on the *William & Sarah*. This was the largest group of Jews to emigrate at one time in colonial America. Except for two families, the Sheftall and the Minis families, all the Jews were Sephardic Jews who had escaped the Inquisition. They had fled Spain and Portugal and gone to London where they worked with a congregation that had been planning to send Jews to the Georgia colony.

On July 11, 1733 the Jewish colonists arrived. Oglethorpe had been given orders by the Trustees, despite their statements of religious freedom, not to give the Jews land. When they arrived, there was a terrible fever outbreak in the new colony and one of the Jews, Dr. Samuel Nunez, was a physician who stopped the epidemic and in Oglethorpe's view, saved the colony. Oglethorpe felt he could not deny them land so he granted to each Jewish man, 50 acres as he had all the other colonists. Many of these Jews did not stay in Savannah long as they feared the Spaniards in Florida would attack and it would be just as it had been in Iberia. After the Spanish were driven out of Florida, some of the early families returned.

The Abraham Minis and Benjamin Sheftall families were Ashkenazic Jews. The first white male child born in Georgia was Phillip Minis born in 1733. The Sheftall Diaries, kept by three generations of the family, are the oldest record of any Jewish congregation in the

2 9

Temple Mickve Israel, Monterey Square

country. The congregation they eventually formed, Mickve Israel, is the third oldest Jewish congregation in the country after New York and Newport, Rhode Island.

The next religious group to arrive were the Salzburgers who arrived in Georgia on March 17, 1734. They had fled religious oppression in Austria and were led by their pastors, Johann Martin Boltzius and Israel Christian Gronau. The Salz-burgers wanted their own settlement apart from the rest of the colonists in Savannah. They established their own community west of Savannah and named it Ebenezer which meant 'Stone of Help'. They laid out their town in a manner similar to the plan of Savannah.

The Salzburgers were very religious and exceptionally hard workers. They were by far the best silkmakers but even they had great difficulty. They completed the first church of any denomination, the Jerusalem Church, in 1741. The old wooden church rotted and in 1770 the present brick building was erected topped by a swan, symbol of their religion. That Jerusalem Church is still in use and is the oldest church building in Georgia. The community was occupied by the British during the Revolutionary War and after that, Ebenezer never regained its former prosperity. The site has been preserved and the Jerusalem Church and a museum about the Salzburgers may be visited.

The Moravians, escaping religious oppression also, arrived in 1736. They came on the ship with Rev. John Wesley who was greatly impressed by their piety. The Moravians set up a school at Irene to educate the Indians. They were however given to evangelizing and the other colonists did not approve. They also would not under any circumstances bear arms, even for defense. These differences resulted

Jerusalem Church, Ebenezer

in the Moravians moving to Pennsylvania by 1740.

The Lutheran congregation in Savannah was originally ministered to by the pastors of Ebenezer. They take the founding date of what is now the Lutheran Church of the Ascension from the April 12, 1741 date when Rev. Boltzius conducted services in Savannah for their congregation. They obtained the land on Wright Square, site of the present church, in 1771. The current building dates to 1844 and was substantially altered in 1875 at which time the stained glass window depicting the Ascension was installed.

In 1755 a Presbyterian Church was established in Savannah and the congregation obtained a grant from King George for a Trust Lot on Ellis Square for the building of the first church for followers of the Doctrines of the Church of Scotland. That first structure would be used by the British as a powder magazine during the Revolutionary War. It was destroyed by fire in 1796. Several other churches were built before 1819 when they erected the first Independent Presbyterian Church on Bull Street at Oglethorpe Avenue. It too was destroyed by fire in 1889 but rebuilt, exactly as before, in 1891.

The Catholics, prohibited in the original charter, came to the area later than many churches. In 1796, Father Oliver LeMercier became the first resident priest. Their first church was on the site of the present Montgomery Street Courthouse. In 1845 the Sisters of Mercy establish St. Vincent's Academy then a convent, orphanage and school. The Cathedral of St. John the Baptist was begun in 1873.

Savannah has very significant African American religious history. Jonathan Bryan owned Brampton Plantation and he provided religious services for his slaves. One preacher who came to Brampton was Rev. George Leile, a slave born in Virginia but given permission by his owner to travel and preach. While visiting the Savannah River plantations, Rev. Leile met and baptized Andrew Bryan, one of Jonathan Bryan's slaves. Andrew Bryan then began to preach to others and on January 20, 1788, at Brampton's barn, the earliest African American Baptist Church in the United States was organized with 67 members.

Andrew Bryan was ordained as minister and slaves from all over the area came to hear him preach. This group formed a congregation and in 1793, obtained land at 575 W. Bryan Street which is said to be the oldest parcel of black owned real estate in the country. In 1794 a church was built on that land and named the First Bryan Baptist Church. This building was replaced by the present building in 1873. The original congregation split in 1832. Some remained members of the First Bryan Baptist Church and others formed what is now the First African Baptist Church. They secured land on Franklin Square and erected their church, still on the same site, in 1859. It was constructed by slaves after they had completed their daily slave duties.

VII

The Thriving Little City

The Georgia Trustees had worked hard and spent a great deal of money on establishing Georgia. They had a 20 year charter but decided that effective one year early, in 1752, they would surrender their charter. Georgia then became a Royal Colony. Oglethorpe left Georgia for the last time on July 22, 1743.

Formal government had never been a hallmark of the colony and even Oglethorpe had no legally mandated duties or responsibilities. The Trustees sent William Stephens to Georgia in 1737 to act as resident secretary to report to them on events. His journal, when published in England, was of great interest. In 1743 Stephens became the first President of Georgia. Henry Parker, for whom Parkersburg is named, was the second president, serving from 1750-52. Patrick Graham was the third president from 1752-54.

In 1754, the first Royal Governor, Captain John Reynolds arrived. He had been given broad powers and he established a Legislature. Noble Jones and James Habersham were among the first legislators. Gov. Reynolds noted that Savannah's buildings were old, wooden, small and rickety. After two years he was replaced by Henry Ellis who seems to have been a genuine character. He spent much of his brief tenure running around under an umbrella with a thermometer dangling from it exclaiming his incredulity at the heat. He moved on to the cooler Nova Scotia and James Wright became the third and last Royal Governor. The wealthiest man in Georgia, he was staunchly pro-British with the coming American Revolution. He would preside over Georgia from 1760-82. Part of the time, during that War, there would be a second Patriot government also ruling Georgia. Archibald Bulloch, an ancestor of President Theodore Roosevelt, was their first president and Button Gwinnett, the second.

Button Gwinnett would achieve further fame as one of Georgia's signers of the Declaration of Independence. The other two signers were Lyman Hall and George Walton. Gwinnett was killed within a year of the signing. He was the looser in a duel with Gen. Lachlan McIntosh. They fought over leadership and strangely, the duel was on land owned by Gov. Wright. Gwinnett's signature is so rare that his is the most prized and expensive of all the signers of the Declaration of Independence. In 1964, a small temple form structure was erected in Colonial Park Cemetery to honor Gwinnett. There was great difficulty in identifying any remains as being those of Gwinnett so his monument says he may have been buried there. Gen. McIntosh who went on to achieve acclaim in the military serving during the Revolution, is also buried in Colonial Park Cemetery.

The first record of a commercial firm was the import/export business established in 1744 by Francis Harris and James Habersham. Habersham came from York, England to head the Bethesda Orphanage. They imported finished products such as china and cloth and exported agricultural products such as lumber, indigo and rice. Rice was a major crop, initially planted right up to the city's doorsteps. Then, fearing disease, a law was passed prohibiting rice planting within a radius of one mile of the town. Owners who took this land out of production were paid $40.00 an acre for doing so. The earliest roads were often privately owned and tolls were charged such as 37 1/2 cents for a loaded wagon and team.

By 1760, Savannah was quite a little town. There were carriages, wigmakers, pubs and even horse races. The original rule of no man owning more than 500 acres had been repealed in 1752 and some citizens owned huge holdings, up to 75,000 acres. By 1752, there were over 200 houses, all but three were wooden and most painted either red or blue.

A 1770 drawing by Gerard deBrahm indicated that the early city was once a walled city. The east wall was located where Lincoln Street is now, the south wall was at Oglethorpe Avenue, and the west side wall was at Jefferson Street. Each wall had two gates but only three of them are shown in use. Those gates were the Trustees Garden Gate on the east, the Great Ogeechee Gate on the south, and the Little Ogeechee gate on the west.

James Johnston began the colony's first newspaper, the *Georgia Gazette*, on April 7, 1763. Johnston was born in Edinburgh, Scotland in 1738 and came to Savannah by way of the Caribbean island of St.

Kitts in 1752. He obtained funds from the local government to buy his printing equipment as there was no printer and the government needed one. His press operated in a building on Broughton Street, just east of

Henry Willink House on St. Julian Street

Drayton Street. He was a Loyalist and so was banished during the Revolution. He always printed what came along for either side so after the War, he was able to reclaim his business. As early as 1801, there were newsboys hawking newspapers on the streets. Johnston died in 1802 and the newspaper ceased. The successor newspaper was the *Columbian Museum* which began in 1803. From 1763 to 1882 forty newspapers came and went. The present *Savannah Morning News* was launched in 1850.

On the eve of the American Revolution, a Bethesda boy, Peter Tondee opened a tavern on the corner of Broughton and Barnard Streets. In this tavern the "Liberty Boys", a group of young patriotic supporters of freedom met and planned their revolutionary activities. Spirits ran high and many fathers retained their loyalty to the King while their sons believed in freedom from England. The stage was set for the Revolution.

VIII

The British Are Coming

In the years prior to the Revolutionary War, Georgians were reluctant to become involved in a rebellion against England. Many causes of discontent found in the other twelve colonies did not exist in Georgia. With the establishment of a thriving plantation system, Georgia fit unusually well into the mercantilism plan of Britain's colonial empire. Possessing only a small shipping industry, little manufacturing, and a large percentage of native born Englishmen as citizens, the colony had few reasons for conflict with Britain.

Another reason was Governor Wright himself. He was an able and respected administrator who maintained good relations with the Executive Council and the small, 29 member Commons House of Assembly. Through his influence, he prevented a Georgia delegation from being sent to the Stamp Act Congress in 1765. He was also able to have the stamped papers used to clear about 60 vessels in Savannah, before a Stamp Act repeal was thought imminent. Georgia was the only colony to do so! After the recently organized Liberty Boys and their supporters held a mass rally in Savannah and burned an effigy of the stamp officer, the stamps and the officer were quietly shipped back to London.

During the ten year interval, a growing constituency in Georgia favored the Patriots (as they styled themselves), mainly inspired by more radical groups in Massachusetts, Virginia and South Carolina. In Georgia a split developed, as it did elsewhere in the colonies, between the wealthier merchant-planter class, who wished to maintain ties with England, and a diverse group of younger and less affluent individuals who wanted independence. The latter group included not only tradesmen and artisans, but also the sons of prominent Loyalists, such as Noble Wymberly Jones, son of Noble Jones, Joseph Habersham, son of James Habersham, and Josiah Tattnall II, son of Josiah Tattnall.

Strong support for the Patriots came from the town of Midway to the south of Savannah. These Congregationalists had maintained strong cultural and religious ties with Massachusetts, where they had lived before settling in Georgia. Two of the three signers of the Declaration of Independence from Georgia came from this small community, and such was the dedication of its residents that the county was renamed "Liberty" in 1777.

Sgt. William Jasper Monument, Madison Square

Although there were many supporters of independence in Georgia, no delegates were sent to the First Continental Congress. Georgia was the only one of the 13 colonies not to do so. The three delegates selected by the First Provincial Congress of Georgia to attend the Second

Continental Congress decided not to go because they felt they did not represent the majority viewpoint. It took news of the Battle of Lexington in April, 1775 to arouse the Georgians. At the July meeting of the Second Provincial Congress, the members redesignated the three representatives and added two more to attend the Second Continental Congress, which was still in session in Philadelphia.

When two British warships were sighted off Tybee in January, 1776, Governor Wright was arrested by a group of Patriots led by Joseph Habersham. Wright escaped the colony shortly afterwards aboard one of the vessels, not to return until after the British recaptured Savannah in 1778. Two months later came the first armed encounter with the British, known as the Battle of the Rice Boats. British warships anchored off Tybee Island running low on provisions attempted to capture vessels loaded with rice which were tied up at a wharf on River Street. The resulting skirmish took place while the Third Provincial Congress was in session in Savannah. Upon hearing gunfire, the delegates quickly adjourned the meeting and agreed to hold the remainder of the sessions in Augusta.

Five delegates were again selected for the next session of the Continental Congress, three of whom, Button Gwinnett, Lyman Hall and George Walton were Georgia's signers of the Declaration of Independence. During the following winter the Provincial Congress busied itself setting up a new constitution and government for the State of Georgia. The system of parishes was abolished and eight counties were created. All were named for English supporters of the American cause, except for Liberty County. Chatham County was named after William Pitt, Earl of Chatham, Member of Parliament and former Prime Minister of England.

Major Charles Lee was placed in charge of the American defense of the southern states, which he inspected in the summer of 1776. Except for Colonel McIntosh and his battalion in Darien, Lee found the Georgians short on money, men, supplies and realism. His now famous quote is, "Upon the whole I shou'd not be surpris'd if they were to propose mounting a body of Mermaids on Alligators..." Not surprisingly the British sent an army to retake Savannah. Most of the military action took place on December 29, 1778. The Americans had rebuilt and strengthened fortifications around the city. They expected the British to attack from the sea, east of Savannah, so they placed most of their troops on the eastern side of Savannah and built a fortification just outside the city across a road which is probably present day Wheaton Street.

Meanwhile, the British misjudged high tide and were unable to land until around 1:00 P.M. when they came ashore at Gerardo's Plantation, near present Fort Jackson. They marched toward Savannah, stopping at 3:00 P.M. to split their forces, taking half their men up the road (Wheaton Street) to Savannah, the other half through swamps and forests around to the southwest side of the city. They were guided by Quash (or Quamino) Dolly, a slave said to have belonged to Governor Wright. The southwest entrance to the city at Ogeechee Road was guarded by a small American force, probably located near present Forsyth Park. As the second group of British attacked the Americans on the southwest side of town, the first group attacked from the east, throwing the untried American soldiers into a panic. They ran through the streets and into streams and rice fields on the west side of town, where many drowned attempting to escape. One casualty was James Jones, mayor of Savannah, said to have been killed on the street that bears his name.

For months afterward local American forces harassed the British without having enough men or resources to retake the city. One of these actions resulted in the recapture of American prisoners being taken to Savannah by the British. They had stopped by a spring to get water, when surprised by Sergeant William Jasper and his men who rescued the Americans. The spring, located at Bay Street and Route 80 in Garden City, was renamed Jasper Spring in his honor.

Less than a year after the disastrous loss of the city, the joint American and French attempt to recapture Savannah known as the Siege of Savannah began. On September 3, 1779 the French fleet under Admiral D'Estaing, consisting of several thousand men and 22 vessels, arrived and anchored off Tybee Island. A meeting was held on Ossabaw Island between the French and Joseph Habersham and other American leaders to discuss the site of the French landing. Beaulieu was selected. (Perhaps the name appealed to the Admiral, since it means beautiful place in French!) By the 16th the French were camped at Greenwich Plantation, which corresponds to present Greenwich Cemetery. Interestingly, among the French were Haitian soldiers including the young Henri Christophe, later to become the leader of Haitian independence. American General Benjamin Lincoln crossed his forces into Georgia at Zubly's Landing, near Ebenezer. He joined General Lachlan McIntosh with his Georgia Continentals and they camped at Cherokee Hill, near present Garden City.

On September 16, without waiting for the Americans, Admiral

D'Estaing sent a demand for the surrender of Savannah in the name of the King of France. Colonel Augustine Prevost, the British commander of Savannah, countered by asking for a 24 hour truce, hoping that the reinforcements that he had sent for from South Carolina would arrive in that time. On the 17th reinforcements arrived in the form of Colonel Maitland and 800 men, cannon and ammunition. He had been able to bring his men into Savannah undetected with the help of slave boatmen who guided them in dense fog through a network of creeks along the coast. Maitland, suffering from yellow fever at the time, could be considered one of the true heroes of the war. Exhausted after the trip, he died of his illness shortly afterwards. Another reinforcement of five British warships sent to Savannah was cleverly captured by an American, Colonel White and six soldiers. They built fires at night and otherwise convinced the British that they were facing an overwhelming force of Americans. White and his men burned the ships, which were anchored in the Ogeechee River.

Count Casimir Pulaski Monument, Monterey Square

During the British occupation, Prevost had built extensive earthworks around the city using slave labor. He replaced the amateurish efforts of the Patriots with effective, well-designed military fortifications. The French and Americans shelled the city for two weeks, hoping to break through the fortifications, then, on October 9, at 2:00 A.M. attacked with a large combined French and American force at the Spring Hill Redoubt which guarded the Augusta Road. After suffering tremendous casualties, over 1,000 men, the Americans and French withdrew. Their losses included Count Casimir Pulaski, cut down by sniper fire early in the battle and the heroic Sergeant Jasper, killed while saving the colors and rallying his men as they stormed the walls of the fortification. The British lost only about 100 men. Spring Hill Redoubt is located near the present Visitors Center in the old Central of Georgia Railroad Passenger Station and marked by a plaque.

Unfortunately the success of the British in Savannah only encouraged the pro-war faction in the British Parliament to successfully press for the continuation of the war. Soon all of the major towns and cities in Georgia were held by the British, and the remnants of the Patriot government fled to Wilkes County, north of Augusta. Here, in the county seat of Heard's Fort, a temporary capital was established.

Within eighteen months, though, the tide had turned against the British. By June, 1781 Augusta had been retaken by American forces, and the capital was established there, only to be transferred to Ebenezer when that town was occupied by American forces a few months later. After the defeat of Cornwallis at Yorktown in October, 1781, General Nathanael Greene moved his army southward to clear the British out of South Carolina. He sent General Anthony Wayne and a force of Continental troops to the Savannah area in the spring of 1782. They effectively controlled the countryside outside of Savannah harassing any British force that left the city, or the small forts at Ogeechee Ferry and Sunbury.

The last major skirmishes took place in May, 1782, when a detachment of Wayne's army defeated the British Lieutenant Colonel Brown and his men. Brown had taken his troops to Harris Bridge over Salt Creek on the Ogeechee Road, where he was supposed to rendezvous with Indian allies, a force of Cherokees under their chief Guristersigo. The Cherokees never showed up, and as the British marched back to Savannah they were attacked around midnight by Wayne's men and suffered major losses of men and arms. The attack took place about four miles from Savannah on Ogeechee Road, probably near present Garrard Avenue. A few days later, the Indians made good on their tardiness by attacking General Wayne and his main force late at night about six miles from Savannah on the Augusta Road. Wayne had just broken camp at Mrs. Gibbon's place, probably Mulberry Hill Plantation, and was heading back to the then state capital at Ebenezer. Wayne and his men succeeded in driving off the Indians, killing Guristersigo and about 30 of his men.

The British surrendered in Savannah on July 11, 1782 and Lt. Colonel James Jackson, known as a great duelist and the man for whom

Fort Jackson is named, was given the honor of accepting the surrender. When the British evacuated the city, they took with them considerable moveable property, including slaves. Many of the slaves, including the preacher George Leile, went willingly with the British because they had been promised their freedom. Unfortunately, except for a few

Delegal Grave Site, Skidaway Island

of the leaders, they were sold into slavery when the ships reached British colonies in the Caribbean. The last recorded confrontation between the Americans and the British came on July 25, after Savannah had been evacuated. A party of foragers from the British Marines landed on Skidaway Island at the Delegal Plantation, looking for food and supplies. A small force of Americans fought them off and burned the plantation buildings in what may have been the final skirmish of the Revolution in Georgia.

Years later, after the Revolution, when Wright retired to England he is said to have felt no ill will toward the former colony of Georgia that he governed, with minor interruptions, for 22 years. Neither did General James Edward Oglethorpe, who is said to have followed with great interest the events taking place on the other side of the Atlantic, always demonstrating sympathy for the people of Georgia. He lived to the age of 97, the only founder of a colony to live to see it become a part of the United States.

IX

The Money Poured In

On the eve of the Revolutionary War, Georgia was beginning to prosper. Population estimates range from 35,000 to 50,000. About 40% of the residents were African American, nearly all slaves. After the Revolutionary War ended, Savannah's population exploded. Organizations were founded which remain today. Churches and homes were built in the finest architectural styles. People, ideas, and the money poured into Savannah.

After his inauguration as the country's first president, George Washington went on a southern tour which included a stop in Savannah that was without doubt, the fanciest party the young colony had ever hosted. Distinguished citizens including Noble Wymberly Jones, Joseph Habersham, John Houston, and General Lachlan McIntosh went out by boat to greet Washington and escort him into town. Washington stayed at Brown's Coffee House, a boarding house long ago destroyed, on the northwest corner of Barnard and State Streets. The major event was a dinner party for 200 people, served by liveried servants, set up along the Savannah River, about where the present Waving Girl statue is located. There were fireworks over the river after dinner. As a thank you gift for the hospitality extended and for their services as escorts, Washington later sent the Chatham Artillery two cannon captured at the Battle of Yorktown. These cannon, later nicknamed "George and Martha" because of their shapes, are now located in a small pavilion on Bay Street, just east of City Hall.

After the War, the properties of men who had been Loyalists were confiscated and given to outstanding Patriots. Of particular importance was the fact that Mulberry Grove Plantation was given to General Nathanael Greene who had been second in command to George Washington. In January, 1783 General Greene and his wife Caty came to Savannah to visit and celebrate. They liked Mulberry Grove and moved there in 1786. Within a short time, General Greene, out

43

inspecting his fields, was overcome with heat stroke and died. He was buried with much pageantry in Colonial Park Cemetery. Caty Greene was left with five children and enormous debts. While aboard ship on a return visit from Washington, D.C., she met Eli Whitney and invited him to Mulberry Grove.

Her lamenting the difficulty of easily removing seed from cotton led Whitney and the Greene children's tutor, Phineas Miller, who would later marry Caty Greene, to invent the cotton gin in 1793. The men got a patent for the gin and marketed them for $500.00 but after anyone watched the machine work, it was easy to duplicate, so they never made money on their invention.

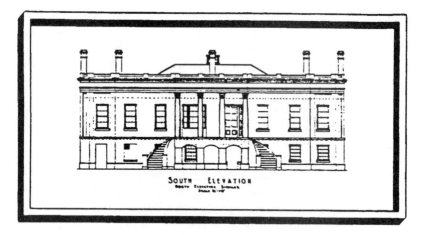

The Hermitage Plantation on the Savannah River

Everyone else made a great deal of money as the gin made growing cotton and preparing it for market an enormously profitable venture. Slavery which was waning was revived as cotton production required many workers. Savannah became a boom town! The world cotton prices would eventually be set in the city and in 1886, the Savannah Cotton Exchange on Bay Street was erected to 'King Cotton'. Cotton would soon be planted everywhere and early accounts say it looked like snow, growing as far as the eye could see in all directions.

Many large plantations developed along the Savannah River, none more prosperous than the Hermitage Plantation of Henry McAlpin. At the Hermitage the Savannah gray bricks that were used to build most

44

of the downrown historic buildings were manufactured, as was much of the decorative iron work. The spur line that McAlpin built to get his bricks down to the River for shipment is said to be one of the oldest railroads in the country. The Hermitage never recovered from the Civil War and in 1935 it was sold to Henry Ford who tore it down and rebuilt it in Richmond Hill. In 1935 the land was leased to Union Bag and Paper Corporation for $1.00. Now called Union Camp, they have remained on the site. Because of their location on the Savannah River, many of the plantations became prime industrial sites. Mulberry Grove is now part of the Georgia Ports Authority; Tweedside/Colerain is now a sugar refinery; Deptford Plantation is the site of the Kemira Co. and Causton's Bluff Plantation is a housing development.

The S.S. Savannah

From the colony's early days, Savannah was a natural shipbuilding site. Much of Savannah's income was from ships bringing goods to the city and Savannah exporting her products. It was only natural then that some merchants including Oliver Sturgess and especially William Scarbrough would back the scheme for a trans-Atlantic steamship. Moses Rogers, a northerner who knew steamboats purchased a ship called 'Fickett's Steam Coffin' which he modified and it became the *S.S.Savannah*. In May, 1818 stock in the venture was sold in Savannah and Scarbrough was the biggest investor. Seeking customers, the ship was sent across the Atlantic and as it approached land, everyone thought the ship was on fire as it was bellowing smoke! Although an object of great curiosity, no deals were struck. The steamship toured England, Ireland, Sweden, Scotland and Russia where the Tsar gave them iron furniture as a remembrance. Since there was no commercial interest, after the ship returned to America, the engine was sold for $1600.00 and the ship put into packet ship service. On November 5, 1821 she was lost off Long Island.

The economic importance of the railroad to Savannah's development was enormous. In 1834, Savannah in an economic slump, commissioned a study about building a railroad to the interior of the state. The report concluded that it was feasible and highly recommended. William Washington Gordon, then mayor of Savannah, was a mover in the development. He was a heavy investor and he became the first president of the Central Railroad and Banking Company which was chartered in 1835. The city bought 5000 shares of stock and donated a five acre tract west of the present Martin Luther King, Jr. Blvd. for the railroad. It was given with the provision that ownership would revert to the city when the railroads no longer used it so in the 1970's, with the end of the railroad era, the city regained ownership.

The actual construction of the lines, 190 miles to Macon, was completed in 1843. As the line extended from Savannah, railroad towns developed. Station One on the Central line is Pooler, named for Robert William Pooler, a friend and associate of Gordon. Bloomingdale was originally Station Two. Other communities developed all along the line. Key to the ongoing success of the Central of Georgia was a man named William Morrill Wadley who was superintendent of the entire line in 1849. He held various positions before going to another company out of state. After the Civil War and the destruction of so much of the railroad, Wadley was urged to return to Savannah and he was named President of the Central of Georgia in 1866. As the line had been such a profit maker and had good credit, they were quickly able to rebuild the line and products, trains, and money started rolling back into Savannah.

The railroad would eventually expand to include steamships in 1872. The company operated the Ocean Steamship Company for many years. The end of the Central of Georgia line came in 1971 when the last train went through the Savannah terminal.

The buildings that survive from this period are the largest collection of intact old railroad buildings in the nation. The largest of the buildings was the passenger terminal at 301 Martin Luther King, Jr. Blvd. It now houses the Savannah Visitors Center and the Savannah History Museum.

South of this building are the historic railroad shops, 19th century railroad repair and manufacturing facilities. Construction of the shops began in 1845 and many of the original structures are still standing including the massive roundhouse and turntable and the 125' tall brick smokestack. The shops are open to the public and are operated by the Coastal Heritage Society. The painted brick building at 227 Martin Luther King, Jr. Blvd. was built in 1856 for offices for the Central Railroad. The red brick building next to it was built in 1888, designed by Alfred Eichberg, also for railroad offices. Both buildings have been restored by and are classrooms for the Savannah College of Art and Design. They also restored the railroad storage sheds behind the Eichberg building that line the parking lot at the Visitors Center.

Anxious to explore all methods of getting products to River Street for shipment, a group of investors developed the Savannah and Ogeechee Canal. The canal ran from the Savannah River, just west of River Street to a point on the Ogeechee River, about a mile west of the present Fort Argyle Road. It opened in 1831 to bring goods from the Ogeechee River basin and western Chatham county to the port of Savannah. In 1848 the canal was renovated and six locks were added. They were built of brick and each was 110' long. Two of the locks can be seen today at the Savannah-Ogeechee Canal Park on Route 204, two miles west of the Route 95 intersection.

The city was prospering but tragedy was about to strike. The Great Fire of 1796 began at City Market on Ellis Square when a stove overheated. There had been no rain and the wooden buildings were very dry so the fire, driven by strong wind, spread rapidly and destroyed over 300 houses. The burned area spanned Bay Street to Oglethorpe Avenue, Barnard to Abercorn Streets. The fire is one of the reasons that Savannah has relatively few 18th century structures. Those that survived the fire include the Pink House on Abercorn Street at Reynolds Square, many of the houses on St. Julian Street, and a few others on the east side of town extending to the old Trustee's Garden area, now the Pirate's House.

The city would suffer two other devastating fires. The Great Fire of 1820 began in Mr. Boone's yard on Franklin Square, again, near City Market. This fire was said to be even worse than the 1796 fire as 463 buildings were lost. There again had been a drought, there was a strong wind, and the fire tore across the city. People, trying to save a few items, put them on empty lots. The city helped each other recover as bakers and grocers gave out provisions. The next major fire, Hogan's

Fire of 1889, began at Hogan's store on Broughton at Barnard Streets. Many buildings including the Independent Presbyterian Church on Bull Street at Oglethorpe Avenue were burned. The church was quickly rebuilt to the 1819 plan.

These great fires led the city to install giant brick cisterns which filled with water used to fight the fires. There were four fire districts and slaves, with their owner's consent, manned them. When the fire bell rang, the first man there got $1.00 and the second, 50 cents. The slaves took great pride in their Fire Companies and provided the best possible fire fighting.

Adrian Boucher, an architect from New York, arrived after the 1796 fire and designed the City Exchange Building in 1799. This was a wooden structure designed in the Georgian style but substantially modified over the years. The building had a tower on it which was manned each night to watch for fires. The City Exchange was destroyed in 1904 to make way for the present City Hall. The bell from the old City Exchange was saved and may be seen on East Bay Street in a replica of the old Exchange Tower. The bell, believed to be the oldest in Georgia, bears the date 1802 and was imported from Amsterdam and hung in the City Exchange in 1804.

The City, in the spirit of patriotic fervor renamed some of the streets after the Revolution. King Street became President Street; Prince Street became State Street; and Duke Street then was Congress Street. Other streets had long before been named to honor South Carolinians who had been helpful to the early colonists. These streets include: Broughton, Drayton, St. Julian, and Whitaker. Bull Street was named for William Bull who surveyed the area. Jones Street was named for John Jones who fell in the Siege of Savannah. Lincoln Street was named for General Benjamin Lincoln. Gaston Street, now home to many gracious inns, was named for William Gaston, a legendary host and philanthropist.

The old colonial town was growing up and prospering and her citizens were ready to build the fine buildings that would reflect their new prosperity.

X

Architectural Gems

The Great Fire of 1796 and the loss of two-thirds of the buildings in the city resulted in many architects and builders coming to Savannah from all over the country as word spread that there was work here. These men would bring with them skills and ideas that would influence the architecture that we still cherish. Their ideas would be modified to the locale so houses were designed with floor to ceiling windows for maximum air circulation. The parlor area was raised to catch any possible breeze. Also, being higher was desirable as they got away from the grit of the sand streets. The kitchens were in the lower level, opening out to the gardens. Many of the houses were built of Savannah gray bricks which were manufactured at the Hermitage Plantation just outside of town. The bricks were inexpensive and not thought fashionable so stucco was used to cover them and often it was scored to resemble stone work. Some of the decorative iron work often used on the houses was also made at the Hermitage. Many of the early builders would teach their slaves woodworking, plaster decorating, and other highly sought after skills. These slaves would then be hired out to others at great profit to the builder.

ISAIAH DAVENPORT

Isaiah Davenport, a master builder, was born in Little Compton, Rhode Island. He arrived in Savannah in 1799 and soon earned a fine reputation as a builder. He was an alderman and quite socially prominent.

He built DAVENPORT HOUSE, 324 East State Street on Columbia Square, as his family home. The Federal house, with a center hall and balanced facade and interior, was typical of the style he had known in Rhode Island. The fine detail, fancy plaster work throughout and the elliptical stairway were a fine showcase for his talents. Davenport died in 1827 and the house changed hands many times. By 1955 it had become a tenement housing many families and was in danger of being torn down for a parking lot. Seven local women, irate about loosing such a historic property, purchased the house, restored it, and opened it as a house museum in 1965. It remains open to the public. The only other surviving structure that is clearly Davenport's work is a small house, moved to State Street, one block east of the Davenport House. Built about 1808, it is called Laura's Cottage and is a private residence.

WILLIAM JAY

A number of Savannah's outstanding houses are built in the Regency style, erected between 1815 and 1820. This grand style with many unique features suited the new 'Merchant Princes'. William Jay, the first professionally trained architect to work in Georgia, was a master

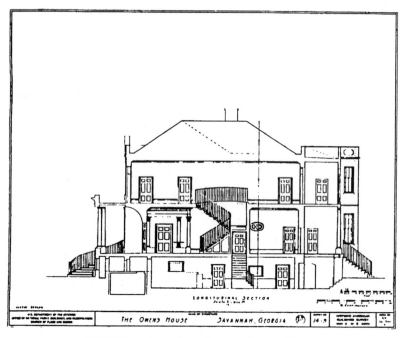

HABS Drawing of the Owens-Thomas House

of Regency grandeur. Jay was born in Bath, England and educated in London. He arrived in Savannah in 1817 to oversee construction of the Richard Richardson house which he designed while still in England. He was related by marriage to Richardson.

The OWENS-THOMAS House that Jay would build at 124 Abercorn Street on Oglethorpe Square is considered by many to be the finest example of Regency architecture in America. Completed in 1819, the house has curved walls and doors, a Jay trademark, a bridge stairway, a parlor ceiling that is flat but appears rounded and unique crown molding throughout. The house was built with interior plumbing, extraordinary for the time. Mr. Richardson suffered financial reverses in the Depression of 1819 and he lost his lovely house. The house was eventually purchased by ancestors of Miss Margaret Thomas who lived in the house until her death in 1951. She bequeathed the house and contents to the Telfair Academy with the request that it be opened to the public as the house museum it is today.

TELFAIR ACADEMY OF ARTS AND SCIENCES, 121 Barnard Street on Telfair Square, was built by Jay for the Alexander Telfair family and completed in 1820. After Telfair's death, the property was inherited by his sisters, Mary and Margaret. Mary Telfair left the property to the Georgia Historical Society with the provision that it be opened to the public and that a large marble tablet be installed on the facade proclaiming the building to be the "Telfair Academy of Arts and Sciences". This was done and extensive changes were made in the interior in the 1880's under the direction of architect Detlef Lienau. It opened as an art museum in 1886 and is one of the oldest in the south. There are typical Jay features including rounded rooms and unique cornices in the period rooms retained on the main floor. They are filled with many Telfair family furnishings.

The WILLIAM SCARBROUGH HOUSE, 41 Martin Luther King, Jr. Blvd., was designed by Jay in 1818 for William and Julia Scarbrough. She was well known for her wonderful parties called "Blowouts" and the couple wanted a house which would reflect his prosperity and provide a fine place for her parties. The house was designed with a sweeping entry with a balcony on the second level and a high curved ceiling which made it appear to be open to the sky. There were rooms on either side of the entry and a ballroom behind. Again Jay used curved walls and doors and distinctive cornices. Scarbrough was a heavy investor in the first trans-Atlantic steamship, the *S.S. Savannah*, which was a technical triumph but not a commercial success. His fortune was lost and ownership of his lovely new residence was gone but the house was purchased by relatives and he continued to live there. The house was later the East Broad Street School for African American children from 1878 to 1964. It then stood vacant until it was restored as a community Bicentennial project in 1976. It was operated by Historic

Savannah Foundation and opened as a house museum. It was sold and closed in 1991 but acquired by the Ships of the Sea Museum in 1994 and again, opened to the public.

SAVANNAH THEATER on Bull Street at Chippewa Square was designed by Jay and built in 1818 in only nine months. Money to build the theater was raised through selling stock in the theater which opened on December 4, 1818. The theater has been remodeled numerous times beginning in the 1850's and ending in the 1950's when it took on its present art deco form.

Jay designed other commercial buildings as well as three other houses which have been demolished before departing Savannah in 1821.

The JULIETTE GORDON LOW BIRTHPLACE, 142 Bull Street at Oglethorpe Avenue, was constructed about 1820 for Mayor James Moore Wayne. The architect of this house is unknown but similarities to the Jay houses suggest that he may have had some involvement. The third floor and side porch were added in 1886. The house was purchased by William Washington Gordon in 1831 and in 1860, his granddaughter, Juliette Gordon, was born in the house. She founded the Girl Scouts of America in 1912. In 1953 the Girls Scouts of the U.S.A. bought the house and in 1956 it was opened to the public as a house museum.

JOHN S. NORRIS

Born in New York, John S. Norris came to Savannah after winning an architectural competition for the design of the U.S. CUSTOM HOUSE, located at the corner of Bull and Bay Streets. Erected in 1852, it was the city's first fireproof building and it was brought in under budget. As was often the case, while in town doing public buildings, architects would accept other commissions. Norris was a master of fancy dwellings and features typical of his houses are hip roofs, bracketed eaves, recessed front doors, often double or even triple sets of doors, unusual windows, often rounded, two story porches, and silver door knobs. Norris would work in Savannah until 1860 when, on the eve of the Civil War, he returned to his home in New York, never to return.

The GREEN-MELDRIM HOUSE, Bull Street at Madison Square,

is one of the finest examples of domestic Gothic architecture in the South. Norris built the house in 1853 for the wealthy merchant Charles Green who had come to Savannah in 1833. The brick exterior was originally covered with stucco. The Gothic exterior detail is repeated inside the house in both plaster and American black walnut. The cost of construction was $93,000.00. In 1864, after the city had surrendered to General William T. Sherman, Green offered his house as Sherman's headquarters saying that he wished to spare any Savannah woman the indignity of having Sherman stay in her home. Others thought he might hope that his hospitality would help him get some of the cotton that the Union Army had confiscated in the city. It was from this house that Sherman sent his telegram to President Abraham Lincoln presenting Savannah to him as a Christmas present. In 1943 this house was purchased by the adjoining St. John's Episcopal Church and it is now the parish house for the church. It is however, often open to the public to tour.

The Andrew Low House, Lafayette Square

The ANDREW LOW HOUSE, 329 Abercorn Street on Lafayette Square, was also designed by Norris. The house was built in 1848 for Andrew Low, a wealthy cotton merchant whose son would marry Juliette Gordon who founded the Girl Scouts of American while living in this house. The house is Italianate and features elaborate brackets and iron work as well as silver door knobs, delicate plaster work, and very high ceilings. The house was purchased in 1928 by the Colonial Dames in the State of Georgia as their headquarters. The house is open to the public for tours.

The MASSIE HERITAGE CENTER, 207 East Gordon Street at Calhoun Square, was designed by Norris as the first public school in the city. It was built with funds donated by Peter Massie for the erection of a school. It was completed in 1856 and now is used for architectural displays and continuing education about Savannah's heritage. It is open to the public.

The MERCER-WILDER HOUSE, 429 Bull Street at Monterey Square, was designed by Norris for General Hugh Mercer and begun in 1860. Work was abandoned when the Civil War began and Norris returned to his home in New York. During the War it is said that the boards from the construction were used by the soldiers to build lean-to shacks in the square. After the War the house was completed by Norris's assistant, DeWitt Bruyn. The elaborate house has been featured in many movies including *Glory*. It is also featured prominently in the book, *Midnight in the Garden of Good and Evil* by John Berendt as it was in this house that the murder, central to the book's plot, occurred. This is a private residence.

CHARLES BLANEY CLUSKEY

Charles Cluskey was an Irish born architect who worked in Georgia beginning in 1830. He was noted for his Greek Revival style. He may have designed the famous Hermitage Plantation for Henry McAlpin.

The CHAMPION-McALPIN HOUSE, located on Barnard Street at Orleans Square, is attributed to Cluskey. It is a fine example of his columned Greek Revival style. It was built in 1843 and acquired by Aaron Champion who left it to his daughter. Her growing family needed more room so in 1880 the top floor with the Mansard roof was added. The house was purchased in 1939 by early preservation activist Alida Harper Fowlkes. At her death in 1985, she left the property to the Society of the Cincinnati in Georgia.

The CONVENT & ACADEMY OF ST. VINCENT de PAUL, Liberty at Abercorn Street, was designed by Cluskey in 1845 for the Sisters of Mercy. It was initially a convent, school, and orphanage.

WILLIAM GIBBONS PRESTON

This architect, from Boston, won an architectural competition for the design of the SAVANNAH COTTON EXCHANGE, 100 E. Bay Street. King Cotton was riding high when plans for this building were drawn. The city specified that the Drayton Street ramp was to be left open so this unique design was the first in the country built over air rights. The building cost $40,000.00 and was completed in 1887. It was erected with iron columns and granite piers supporting it but leaving the ramp open. It was constructed of red brick and terra cotta. Preston also designed the griffin stationed in front spewing water from its mouth. The building is now occupied by Solomon's Lodge #1 which dates back to the earliest colonial days. The building is occasionally opened for the public to tour.

Preston also designed the OLD CHATHAM COUNTY COURTHOUSE on Bull Street at Wright Square. Built in 1889, this structure underwent total renovation in 1990 and is now Chatham county offices.

The SAVANNAH VOLUNTEER GUARDS ARMORY, 340-44 Bull Street at Madison Square, was designed by Preston in 1893. It is distinguished by its heavy red brick Romanesque styling and by the cannon that stand guard on either side of the entrance. It is now a building of the Savannah College of Art and Design.

Architect HYMAN WITCOVER designed the present Savannah City Hall in 1905. Dominating the skyline with its gold dome, it is located on Bay Street at Bull Street. His design originally included more chariots and horses on the exterior but money was short so the design was modified.

Architecturally unique to Savannah is the 40' bluff area spanning Bay Street to the Savannah River, the site where Oglethorpe landed. The top side of that bluff is the present Bay Street and the downside of the bluff is River Street. In the days when cotton was king, cotton factors or brokers had their offices on the top side, the Bay Street side. A lane called Factor's Walk ran between the bluff and the buildings. Small walking bridges arch over Factor's Walk to connect the second and third storey offices with the sidewalks of Bay Street. These ranges of buildings were designed by many different architects and today they serve a variety of functions from city offices to historic inns and restaurants.

All along Bay Street there are steep stairs or cobblestone ramps that lead down to River Street. The streets and supporting walls were built of ships ballast. Originally these ramps were white sand and from the earliest days of the colony were heavily traveled, making getting stuck in the sand with a loaded cart almost inevitable. Thus, the ramps and adjoining streets were among the first paved streets in the city.

Factor's Walk

In the 1970's the old warehouses were renovated. A brick walkway was installed all along the river with benches and mini-parks. ROUSAKIS RIVERFRONT PLAZA, named for longtime Mayor John P. Rousakis, is in the center of the area.

In the mid-town area there are many notable houses including the very early Drouillard Plantation House built in 1799. It is now the Cottage Shop at 2422 Abercorn Street. A true victorian charmer is the "Gingerbread House" on Bull Street at 36th Street. It was built in 1899 by German-born grocer Cord Asendorf. His daughter Sophie lived there until 1976.

XI

Squares Beautiful Squares

James Edward Oglethorpe's original city plan established a pattern of open spaces, most about one acre, called city squares. Around these squares the houses, churches and public buildings were erected. Johnson Square is the first square laid out by Oglethorpe in 1733. The last square, laid out in 1851, is Whitefield Square. There were originally 24 squares and all but two of them remain. The lost squares are on Montgomery Street: Elbert Square, named for Revolutionary War General Samuel Elbert, across from the Civic Center and Liberty Square, now a small space at the Chatham County Courthouse 'Flame of Freedom' site. Another square, Ellis Square retains its position but is now covered with a parking deck. All the squares are on north/south streets. The squares by street are as follows:

BULL STREET SQUARES from north (Bay Street) to south: Johnson Square, Wright Square, Chippewa Square, Madison Square and Monterey Square

ABERCORN STREET SQUARES from north (Bay Street) to south: Reynolds Square, Oglethorpe Square, Lafayette Square and Calhoun Square

BARNARD STREET SQUARES from north (Bay Street) to south: Ellis Square (now a parking deck), Telfair Square, Orleans Square, Pulaski Square, and Chatham Square

HABERSHAM STREET SQUARES from north (Bay Street) to south: Warren Square, Columbia Square, Troup Square, and Whitefield Square

HOUSTON STREET SQUARES from north (Bay Street) to south: Washington Square, Greene Square and Crawford Square

The squares were laid out and named much earlier than their centerpiece monuments so the squares never have the same name as the monument in the center. Over the years, some of the squares have been renamed to honor a more contemporary citizen or event. Often squares were named to honor military heroes or victories. Many of the monuments were erected in the Victorian period when it was fashionable to honor early heroes. Often patriotic organizations would spearhead such a project. Money for the monuments was often raised by a lottery. When a cornerstone was laid or a monument unveiled, grand festivities were held on the squares celebrating the occasion. It was the custom that monuments faced the enemy so Oglethorpe's statue faces south as the Spaniards in Florida were his foe. The soldier atop the Confederate monument in Forsyth park likewise faces north.

CALHOUN SQUARE
This square was laid out in 1851, one of the last squares. It is on Abercorn Street and the cross streets are Taylor and Gordon. It was named for John C. Calhoun, a well known South Carolina politician who had visited the city while he was Secretary of War in 1819. Massie School, named for Peter Massie who gave $10,000.00 to establish the school, is on the south side of the square. Designed by John S. Norris, the school opened in 1856, and it is considered the oldest school in Georgia in continuous operation. It is now the Massie Heritage Center, operated by the public schools to enhance knowledge of early Savannah. There are displays on architecture and a 19th century classroom. It is open to the public. Wesley Monumental Church is on the western Trust Lot. Dedicated in 1890, funds for the church were raised through international subscription to honor the Wesley brothers. There are fifteen memorial windows including the Wesley Window depicting John and Charles Wesley with the inscription, "My Parish".

CHATHAM SQUARE
This square, located on Barnard Street between Taylor and Gordon, was laid out in 1847. The square and our county were named for William Pitt, the Earl of Chatham, an early friend of the colony. Gordon Row, a row of fifteen four story townhouses built as rental housing, extends from the southeast corner to Whitaker Street. Across the square is the Barnard Street School, originally a public elementary school, now one of the buildings of the Savannah College of Art and Design.

CHIPPEWA SQUARE

This square is on Bull Street and the cross streets are Hull and Perry. Laid out in 1815, this square was named for the Battle of Chippewa in the War of 1812. The Savannah Theater on the east side of the square is the much altered theater designed by William Jay and completed in just nine months in 1818. The First Baptist Church completed in 1833 is on the western Trust Lot. Next to the church at 17 W. McDonough Street is the Moses Eastman House designed by Charles Cluskey in 1844 with a third floor added in 1911.

Oglethorpe Monument, Chippewa Square

The monument to the city's founder, James Edward Oglethorpe, is in the center of the square. In 1901 several patriotic organizations began planning for the monument. The prominent Daniel Chester French and his associate Henry Bacon were commissioned to design the monument. They also did the seated Lincoln Monument in Washington, D.C. Done in bronze, Oglethorpe is attired in the uniform of a British general of his period. The statue was unveiled, amid much celebration, in 1910.

COLUMBIA SQUARE

This square is located on Habersham Street and the cross streets are State and York. It was laid out in 1799 and given the poetic name for the United States. On the northwest corner of the square is the Davenport House, built by master builder Isaiah Davenport, as his family home. In 1955 this house had deteriorated and was a tenement. When it was threatened with demolition, seven women raised the funds and bought the residence. They then restored it and opened it as the house museum it remains today. From this activity, the Historic Savannah Foundation began. On the west side of the square is the Kehoe House, once owned by Joe Namath, now a luxury inn. Built in 1893 for William Kehoe who owned the local iron works, much of the exterior trim is cast iron. In the 1990's much private restoration activity was done in this area including the wooden houses surrounding this square which were completely redone. The Universalist Church on the south side of the square was the former Sheftall house and was moved to this square.

The centerpiece fountain on the square is the Wormsloe Fountain, placed in the square in 1970 as a memorial to Wymberly and Augusta DeRenne, descendants of Noble Jones, one of the most distinguished of the original colonists.

CRAWFORD SQUARE

Located on Houston Street with the cross streets Hull and Perry, this square is the only one still fenced as all squares were at one time. Crawford Square was laid out in 1841 and named to honor William Harris Crawford who was Secretary of the Treasury in the administration of President James Madison.

ELLIS SQUARE

Now covered by a parking deck, this square on Barnard Street with cross streets Bryan and Congress, is the gateway to the City Market area of shops and restaurants. Ellis is one of the first squares, laid out in 1733. Named for Royal Governor Henry Ellis, it was often referred to as Market Square as from earliest days, it was the site of markets. There was a huge old City Market building here which sold all manner of delicacies. It was demolished in 1954 and this act outraged citizens and awakened preservationists who began to work to stop further destruction.

FRANKLIN SQUARE

This square is at the west end of City Market and is on Montgomery Street, the cross streets are Bryan and Congress. It was named for Benjamin Franklin, the colony's agent in London, and was laid out in 1791. For many years it was the site of the city's water tower so was

Franklin Square "Old Water Tower Square", c. 1850

called Water Tower Square. The First African Baptist Church on the western Trust Lot was built by slaves in 1859 and has remarkable stained glass windows depicting important figures in the church's history. There are floors with holes in a decorative pattern that provided air for the slaves often hidden underneath as well as pews marked by men with their African symbols. The church is often open to tour.

GREENE SQUARE

This square is on Houston Street and the cross streets are State and York. It was laid out in 1799 and was named to honor General Nathanael Greene, Revolutionary War hero. The Second African Baptist Church on the western Trust Lot dates from 1802. It was from this church that General William T. Sherman issued Field Order #15 which promised the newly freed slaves "Forty acres and a mule". The former Savannah Female Orphan Asylum built in 1801, is on the north side of the square.

JOHNSON SQUARE

This, the city's first square, is located on Bull Street with the cross streets Bryan and Congress. Laid out in 1733, the square was named for Robert Johnson, Royal Governor of South Carolina when Georgia was founded. Here the colonists had their well and oven. Oglethorpe laid aside the southeast Trust Lot for the Anglican Church, now Christ Church Episcopal. The present church, on the original site, dates to 1838 but it sustained substantial damage in an 1897 fire. Some walls and the foundation were saved and the church was rebuilt as we see it today. This is now the banking square. The tallest office building is the First Union Building on the northeast corner. It has fifteen stories and was built in 1912.

The Nathanael Greene Monument is the centerpiece of this square. General Greene was second in command to George Washington during the Revolutionary War and was given Mulberry Grove Plantation in Savannah for his service to the country. The cornerstone for his monument was laid in 1825 by the Marquis de Lafayette. The Egyptian Obelisk was designed by noted architect William Strickland in 1829. Made of New York white marble and 50' tall, it was an object of controversy as it was considered too plain. Responding to chronic complaints, bronze plaques were added in 1886 making it less plain, and more acceptable. In 1901, members of the Society of the Cincinnati of Rhode Island, feeling that their native son should be buried beneath his monument, arranged for the remains of General Greene and his son to be moved from Colonial Park Cemetery and buried under the monument.

LAFAYETTE SQUARE

This square is on Abercorn Street and the cross streets are Harris and Charlton. Laid out in 1837, it was named for the Marquis de Lafayette. There is a lovely fountain in the center of the square. The Andrew Low House, located on the west side of the square, is owned by the Colonial Dames in Georgia and it is their headquarters. It was built in 1849 and was designed by John S. Norris. This was the home of Juliette Gordon Low after she married William Low. She was living in this house in 1912 when she founded the Girls Scouts of America. The group's first meetings were held in the carriage house that adjoins this property. This house museum is open to the public. Across the square, on the southeast side, is the Flannery O'Connor House where the writer spent her childhood. There is a historic marker in front of the house noting its significance. It is open weekends. St. John the Baptist Catholic Cathedral is located on the north side of the square. It adjoins St. Vincent's Academy, still a convent and school for girls, it opened in 1845. The Gothic Cathedral, begun in 1873, was completed in 1896 when the twin spires were finished. Fire soon destroyed much of the original structure. It was rebuilt in 1899. The Cathedral is open daily for visits.

MADISON SQUARE

This square is on Bull Street and the cross streets are Harris and Charlton. It was laid out in 1837 and was named to honor President James Madison. St. John's Episcopal Church on the western Trust Lot was completed in 1853. In the Gothic style, it was designed by Calvin Otis of New York. The chimes of St. John's began with the donation of eight bells and now there are 47 bells in the carillon. In 1943 the adjoining property, now known as the Green-Meldrim House was acquired by the church and it serves as their parish house. This Gothic Revival house with its unusual oriel windows, was designed by John S. Norris in 1853 for wealthy merchant, Charles Green. It cost $93,000.00 to build. General Sherman stayed here in 1864 during his occupation of Savannah. When not in use by the church, the house is open to the public. The Francis Sorrel House built in 1841 and attributed to Charles Cluskey is on the northwest corner. Across the square, on the south side, the large red brick Romanesque building was erected for the Savannah Volunteer Guards in 1893. Still guarded by giant cannon, it was designed by William Gibbons Preston and is a building of the Savannah College of Art and Design.

In the center of the square there is the Jasper Monument, unveiled at a gala party in 1883. It honors Sergeant William Jasper who was renowned for saving the colors in several battles including the 1779 Revolutionary Battle of Savannah. He was killed in that battle. The monument of bronze and marble was designed by Alexander Doyle.

MONTEREY SQUARE

Also located on Bull Street, the cross streets for this square are Taylor and Gordon. From the square, there is a fine view of the fountain in Forsyth Park. Laid out in 1847, the square was named for one of the battles in the Mexican War in which the local Irish Jasper Greens participated. All but one of the buildings (United Way Building) around this square are original. Temple Mickve Israel on the eastern Trust Lot is Gothic and was designed for the congregation by D.M. Foley of Savannah and completed in 1878. Behind the Temple, on Wayne Street, is a museum, open to the public, which features the history of the congregation which dates from 1733 and is the third oldest Jewish congregation in the country. Across the square is the Mercer-Wilder House, designed by John S. Norris and begun in 1860 but not completed until after the Civil War. It has been featured in many movies and is the residence where the murder occurs in the book *Midnight in the Garden of Good and Evil.*

Mercer-Wilder House on Monterey Square

In the center of Monterey Square is the monument to Count Casimir Pulaski, the highest ranking foreign officer to die in the American Revolution. He died in the Battle of Savannah in 1779 and was buried at sea. The cornerstone for this monument and the Greene monument were laid in 1825 by the Marquis de Lafayette. Funds for the monument were raised through a lottery. The monument, designed by Polish-American Robert E. Launitz, was executed in Italy.

OGLETHORPE SQUARE

This square on Abercorn Street has the cross streets State and York. Laid out in 1742, it honored James Edward Oglethorpe, the founder of Georgia. In the early days, it was called 'Upper New Square' and was the site of many lovely mansions. On the northeast Trust Lot, one of them, the Owens-Thomas House survives. Considered the finest example of Regency architecture in the country, it was designed by William Jay and finished in 1819. It is now a house museum, open to the public. Across the square there is the former Marine Hospital built in 1907, now an urban Health Center. There is a Moravian Marker is this square commemorating the service of the Moravians who were in Savannah from 1736 to 1740.

ORLEANS SQUARE

Located on Barnard Street, the cross streets are Hull and Perry. Laid out in 1815, this square was named to honor the United States victory at the Battle of New Orleans in 1815. The imposing house with the massive columns on the east side of the square is the Champion-McAlpin House, built in 1844 for Aaron Champion and attributed to architect Charles Cluskey. The third floor Mansard roof was added in the late 1800's when the growing McAlpin family needed more space. The house is now owned by the Society of the Cincinnati in the State of Georgia. Several other outstanding houses were on this square but were demolished for civic buildings. The current Civic Center was completed in 1970. The German Societies placed a fountain and benches in the center of this square in the late 1980's.

PULASKI SQUARE

This square is on Barnard Street and the cross streets are Harris and Charlton. It was laid out in 1837 and named to honor Polish Count Casimir Pulaski, the highest ranking foreign officer to die in the American Revolution. On the northwest corner there is an example of new housing done in the old style. It was built in 1993 and resembles the Bernard Constantine house on the west side of the square which was built in 1845.

REYNOLDS SQUARE

This square is on Abercorn Street and the cross streets are State and York. It is one of the original squares, laid out in 1733 and was named for Georgia's first Royal Governor, John Reynolds. This was the site of Rev. John Wesley's parsonage when he was Anglican minister to the colony in 1736. There was a Filature House, the center of the colony's silkmaking effort, on the northeast Trust Lot. After silkmaking was abandoned, it served as a meeting house until it was destroyed by fire in 1839. The Pink House, on the west side of the square, was built as the Habersham family home in 1789. One of the few buildings to survive the fire of 1796, it is now a restaurant. Legend says that it is pink because the brick bled through the stucco.

In the center of the square there is a monument to Rev. John Wesley which was erected by the Methodists of Georgia in 1969 to honor their founder. The bronze statue atop a black marble pedestal depicts Wesley in a preaching stance. The sculptor was Marshall Daugherty.

TELFAIR SQUARE
From 1733 when it was laid out until 1883, this square on Barnard Street between York and State was named St. James's Square. It was one of the most fashionable residential areas. It was renamed to honor the Telfair family. Their family home, designed by William Jay and completed in 1820, is now the Telfair Academy of Arts and Sciences. It is one of the oldest art museums in the south and is open to the public and handicapped accessible. Next to it is the Trinity Methodist Church, built in 1848 and designed by John B. Hogg. Across the square are the Low Federal Buildings, erected in the 1980's often referred to as the bathroom tile buildings, only lacking shower heads!

TROUP SQUARE
This square, laid out in 1851, is located on Habersham Street between Charlton and Harris. It is named for George Michael Troup, Governor and U.S. Senator. On Charlton Street, on the east side, there are the McDonough Row houses built in 1882. The restoration of this row of buildings was one of the first projects completed in the 1960's when federal funds became available for restoration. An example of the modern iron work done by Ivan Bailey may be seen on the sunflower door on the house on the southwest corner of the square. The Savannah Baptist Center, a church moved to this site in 1860, is on the west Trust Lot. It is known as the 'Jingle Bells Church' as the composer, James L. Pierpont, was the music director when the piece was written. In the center of the square there is an Armillary Sphere, an ancient astronomical device. The sphere was done in the 1970's. Near it is an elaborate fountain for dogs.

WARREN SQUARE
Laid out in 1791, this square is also on Habersham Street and the side streets are Bryan and Congress. It is named for General Joseph Warren who was killed in the Battle of Bunker Hill. This square has been the site of considerable restoration activity in the mid-1990's as many of the wooden houses have been totally redone.

WASHINGTON SQUARE
This square is on Houston Street between Congress and Bryan Streets. It was named for George Washington. The Seaman's House and Chapel are on the west side of the square. Around this square and on St.Julian Street, going west to Warren Square, are some of the oldest houses in the city.

WHITEFIELD SQUARE
This square, on Habersham Street between Taylor and Gordon, was the city's last square, laid out in 1851. It was named for Rev. George Whitefield, fourth minister of the colony. An internationally known evangelist, he established the Bethesda Orphanage in 1740. The centerpiece gazebo is in keeping with the architecture of this area as Victorian wooden houses predominate. The First Congregational Church built in 1895, founded by missionaries who had come to teach at the Beach Institute, is on the western Trust Lot. The modern Red Cross building and the Rose of Sharon apartments are on the north side.

WRIGHT SQUARE
One of the oldest squares, Wright Square is on Bull Street between State and York. It was laid out in 1733 and originally named Percival Square for Viscount Percival, the Earl of Egmont. It was renamed to honor James Wright, Georgia's last Royal Governor. It was commonly called "Courthouse Square" as from earliest days there was a courthouse here. The present yellow brick one was designed by William Gibbons Preston and renovated in 1992 for continued use as county offices. Next to it is the Lutheran Church of the Ascension, so named for its beautiful window installed in 1878. Across the street is the U.S.Post Office and Federal Building, erected in 1895. It features panels around the top of the structure of all types of marble quarried in Georgia.

The monument in the square was erected by the Central of Georgia Railroad to honor their founder, William Washington Gordon. Designed by Van Brunt and Howe of Boston of red granite, it was dedicated in 1884. To accommodate the Gordon work, the monument to Tomochichi which had been erected in 1739 by the early settlers, was destroyed. In 1899, the Colonial Dames in Georgia placed the huge boulder of Georgia granite on the southeast corner of the square. It is dedicated to Tomochichi, Mico of the Yamacraw Indians.

OTHER GREEN SPACES AND MONUMENTS

FORSYTH PARK is immediately south of the Landmark Historic District and is a 20 acre park bounded by Gaston Street to the north, Park Avenue to the south, Drayton Street to the east and Whitaker Street to the west. A private citizen, William Hodgson, feeling that the city should have a large park, initially set aside some of the space that is now Forsyth Park. In 1851, the park was expanded to its present 20 acre size. It is named for John Forsyth a Georgia Governor. The centerpiece fountain was erected in 1858.

The CONFEDERATE MONUMENT centered in the park behind the fountain, was dedicated in 1874 to honor the Confederate soldiers. It was made in Canada of Canadian materials and brought to Savannah by ship so as to never touch Yankee soil. Atop the monument is a bronze soldier done by David Richards.

EMMET PARK
This area, on the east end of Bay Street, was named for Irish patriot Robert Emmet. The old Harbor Light was placed here in 1852 to warn those coming up the Savannah River of the old vessels scuttled in the water. In this area there is a Celtic Cross and the Vietnam Memorial.

WAVING GIRL
On the far eastern end of River Street there is a statue of the Waving Girl. It commemorates Florence Martus, the sister of the lighthouse keeper who began in 1887 waving at every ship that entered or left the port of Savannah. She waved at every vessel for 44 years and reportedly never missed one ship. Through this dedication, she became internationally known as sailors throughout the world told about her. The statue to her memory was done by sculptor Felix de Weldon.

XII

Savannah In Repose

COLONIAL PARK CEMETERY may be entered through the large gate at the corner of Oglethorpe Avenue and Abercorn Street. The gate was erected by the Daughters of the American Revolution. This was the city's public burial ground from 1750 to 1853. The unusual above ground brick structures in various architectural styles are family vaults. Other monuments were erected to resemble a table with the engraving of remembrance on the tabletop portion with fancy legs holding it aloft. There is a small temple form building erected in

Brick Family Vault, Colonial Cemetery

the 1960's to honor Button Gwinnett, one of three Georgia signers of the Declaration of Independence. The man who killed Gwinnett in a duel, Revolutionary War General Lachlan McIntosh, is also buried in this cemetery. Many other early leaders are buried here including the following: William Scarbrough, Joseph Habersham, and Archibald Bulloch, great-great grandfather of President Theodore Roosevelt. During the Civil War, Union soldiers occupying Savannah camped in the cemetery and for amusement, some of the gravestones were altered to show someone dying before they were born!

LAUREL GROVE CEMETERY was dedicated in 1853 to replace Colonial Park Cemetery. It is on Anderson Street, just west of Martin Luther King, Jr. Blvd. Laurel Grove is the former Springfield Plantation which spread from Louisville Road at the present Visitors Center to Ogeechee Road. Once planted with rice and then cotton, the area was given to the city in 1840 for use as a cemetery.

Laurel Grove was laid out like the historic district with little green areas and wide lanes for the carriages as it was quite fashionable to come riding out to the area on Sunday and visit not only the deceased but one another. Some mausoleums even had porch like areas and relatives would bring chairs and sit there each Sunday greeting people. There is extraordinary iron work around many of the graves. The mausoleums were designed in various architectural styles, often done by the most famous architects working in Savannah over the years.

Just inside the gate is a map of the cemetery and brochures entitled "A Tour of Savannah's Necropolis" which gives brief information about some of the most famous people buried here. There is a large soldiers' burial field as well as the graves of many early Savannahians including the following: Juliette Gordon Low, founder of the Girl Scouts; Florence Martus, the Waving Girl; James Pierpont, composer of "Jingle Bells"; members of the Mackay family popularized by the novels of Eugenia Price; and Isaac Axson, pastor of the Independent Presbyterian Church who married his granddaughter Ellen Axson to future President Woodrow Wilson. Early black leaders are buried in the south section of the cemetery. Rev. Andrew Bryan is buried here as are members of the Deveaux family.

BONAVENTURE CEMETERY is situated on a bluff overlooking the Wilmington River and because of the beauty of the site and the lush vegetation, it was often said that it was better to be buried in Bonaventure than be alive anywhere else! The cemetery is divided into several sections.

The older section was once Bonaventure Plantation, home of Colonel Mulryne. In 1760 it was passed on his daughter and her husband Josiah Tattnall. It remained in the family until 1847 when the land was sold for use as a cemetery. The earliest graves are those of the Tattnall family and soldiers killed in the Revolutionary War.

One of the most beautiful mansions in the south once stood in what is now the Greenwich Section of the cemetery. Built about 1900 by Spencer Shotter and purchased by Dr. H. Torrey in 1917, the house had 40 lavishly furnished rooms but it too was destroyed by fire. As one enters main gate, there is a large tomb with the name Gaston on it. This is the Strangers Tomb where persons who died in Savannah were placed until arrangements were made for their return to their home communities. This vault was erected by his friends as a memorial to William Gaston who in life was a legendary host and philanthropist.

Little Gracie, Bonaventure Cemetery

Noble Jones, one of the first colonists, and his descendants are buried here, as well as composer Johnny Mercer and writer Conrad Aiken. There is also a memorial to Gracie, daughter of the manager of the old Pulaski Hotel who always greeted hotel visitors. She died of pneumonia at age six. Often toys and flowers are placed at her grave. Her monument, carved life size from a photograph, was done in 1894 by John Walz.

In addition to these three major cemeteries, there are a host of smaller ones, each with its own interesting story to tell. All of these cemeteries are on private land and not open to the general public.

BRYAN CEMETERY is on the Savannah River at the location of Brampton Plantation. Within the cemetery's brick enclosure is the 1788 mausoleum of Jonathan Bryan, Revolutionary War patriot. Other grave markers and table top tombs range in date from 1783-1862. The cemetery is of interest in African American history as it marks the location of Brampton Plantation, where Andrew Bryan, one of the slaves, founded the first black church in America in 1788.

JEWISH CEMETERY and SHEFTALL CEMETERY both date from the late colonial period. The first Jewish burying ground of the colonial period was in what is now the median on Oglethorpe Avenue at Bull Street and is identified by a bronze marker. The JEWISH CEMETERY, south of the Central of Georgia Railroad complex, covers five acres and is surrounded by a high tabby wall. It was opened around 1760, and is mentioned as a landmark during the Siege of Savannah in 1779. The cemetery continued in use through the 19th century with many of the larger monuments dating from this period. The SHEFTALL CEMETERY for family members is nearby.

CHEROKEE HILL AND DOTSON CEMETERIES are located west of Port Wentworth on Cherokee Hill. CHEROKEE HILL CEMETERY is a large black cemetery with burials dating from the late 19th century. Near it is the smaller white DOTSON CEMETERY, which is no longer in use. It appears to be the older of the two, with tombstones and table top tombs dating from 1818 to the mid 20th century. It is believed that Cherokee Hill was named during the Revolutionary War because it was the camping place of a band of Cherokee Indians, allies of the British. Not far from Cherokee Hill is the AIRPORT CEMETERY. When the Savannah International Airport was constructed, one of the runways went through another Dotson family cemetery. All the graves were relocated except two, those of Richard and Catherine Dotson. They remained and a bronze memorial plaque was placed in the cement runway directly above their final resting place.

NORTH SALEM BAPTIST CHURCH CEMETERY was established around the time that the church was organized in 1829 on land donated by the Keller family. It is located in the northern part of the county, close to the Effingham County line. The earliest part of the cemetery, dating from the first half of the 19th century, appears to be the Keller family plot which is surrounded by a low brick wall. Coldbrook Plantation House, featured on the cover of *Savannah Spectres* by Margaret Wayt DeBolt, was built by the Kellers. Originally situated only a few miles from the church, the house has since been moved to a location in McIntosh County.

BETHEL BAPTIST CHURCH CEMETERY also began as a family cemetery. Here the land for the church and cemetery was donated by the Gould family, and the earliest grave is said to be that of Ann Gould who died around 1848. An oak avenue once led from the Gould home, known as Bethel, to the church. Down this road, bread and wine both made at the plantation, were brought to the church for communion services. A one room schoolhouse, Bethel School, was once located near the church, and a member of the family, Carrie E. Gould taught at the school for 47 years. In her honor, the public school closest to the Bethel Community, at Silk Hope, was named Gould Elementary.

ISLE OF HOPE METHODIST CHURCH CEMETERY is on Parkersburg Road at the Isle of Hope. During the Civil War, the church was fortified with four cannon in the front yard, and later used as a hospital for wounded Confederate soldiers. The cemetery contains 33 soldiers' graves, mostly those of volunteers from Effingham County. In 1984 the church structure burned to the ground, but was rebuilt as a replica the following year. The original pews, which had been removed prior to the fire, can still be seen inside the church. Many are carved with the soldiers' names or initials.

OLD EASTSIDE CEMETERY is located on the marsh at the end of Alaska Street not far from Greenwich Cemetery. Although the earliest tombstone is dated 1874, it was probably in use prior to that time by the black community of east Savannah. Since 1935 the cemetery, with over 200 gravesites, has been cared for by the Eastside Community Club. Older residents recall New Orleans-style funerals with brass bands following horse drawn hearses to the cemetery. Black horses are said to have pulled the hearses of the elderly, while white horses pulled the hearses of those who died young.

XIII

The Great Unpleasantness

On the eve of the Civil War, most of the houses we now admire in the historic district were in place. The last of the city's 24 squares was laid out in 1851. The Georgia census of 1860 showed there were 598,000 white persons and 465,000 black persons of whom 3500 were "free persons of color".

Meetings were held day and night, especially around Johnson Square urging secession. Many evenings there were torchlight parades. Draped across the Nathanael Greene monument was a banner declaring "Do Not Tread on Me". Many supporters wore rosettes made from palmettoes. The vote to secede was taken at the state capital in Milledgeville on January 19, 1861.

Georgia took control of Fort Jackson and Fort Pulaski. Ft. Pulaski was a mess, overgrown with weeds, so much effort was expended preparing it for use. Ft. Jackson was bolstered. Ft. Cheves was erected across the Savannah River. The largest of the earthenwork fortifications were put in place at Causton's Bluff, renamed Ft. Bartow. For interior defenses, a four and a half mile arc extending from the Savannah River to Laurel Grove Cemetery was built, mostly by slaves. At all water entrances to the city, fortifications were manned including four at the Isle of hope, six at Skidaway Island, and others at Rose Dhu, Beaulieu, Vernonburg, Whitemarsh and Wilmington Islands. Ft. McAllister, an earthenwork defense on the high ground at the mouth of the Ogeechee River was begun in 1861. By November, 1861 Union forces, having taken Hilton Head, were blocking the river. General Robert E. Lee whose first assignment after graduating West Point was at Ft. Pulaski working on the drainage, returned to inspect the area. He felt that Ft. Pulaski could be held but that the Confederates should evacuate Tybee Island as they could not hold that area. This would prove a fatal error.

Soon after the area was evacuated, Union men began working at night secretly building fortifications out on the marshes from which the Fort could be bombarded. The Confederate forces refused to surrender as they felt no cannon had sufficient range to reach them. What they did not know was that a new weapon, rifled cannon, had been developed. On April 10, 1862 the bombardment began. This was the first use of rifled cannon and their range greatly exceeded that of any previously known device. Soon there were holes in Ft. Pulaski's

Fort Pulaski

seven and a half foot thick brick walls, once thought impenetrable. After 30 hours of bombardment, Colonel Charles Olmstead, Confederate commander at the Fort, surrendered. Union forces would occupy the Fort until the War ended. The occupation of the Fort effected a total blockade of the city from then on.

The city was sealed off and within a short time, there was nothing in the stores. Ladies noted that a dress which could have been purchased for $9.00 would cost $195.00. In 1864 four shad cost nearly $30.00 that would have cost only 50 cents before the War. The soldiers stationed in the city complained about the fleas and mosquitoes as big an hummingbirds. Malaria and measles ravaged the troops many of whom were stationed in Savannah awaiting orders.

No southern port turned out more ships than Savannah, many made at the shipyard of Henry Willink. Three ironclads were made in Savannah: the *Atlanta,* the *Savannah,* and the *Georgia.* There was a Ladies Gunboat Association that raised $75,000.00 to build an ironclad, the *Georgia* that was so unseaworthy that it had to be towed to Ft. Jackson where it remained as a defense. It was scuttled as Sherman approached and remains in the water near Ft. Jackson.

Life in the city was very difficult. Food was expensive and in short supply. Nearly every family had lost loved ones and most women were in black mourning clothes. Few men or boys were left in the city. General William T. Sherman had been burning his way to the coast and arrived at Ft. McAllister, just south of the city, in December, 1864. Sherman sent a letter demanding that Savannah surrender. No reply was sent immediately and Sherman waited, as he felt the city was nearly starved so why risk his troops. In the meantime, those Confederate forces still in the city built a pontoon bridge across to Hutchison Island and escaped to fight elsewhere. Dr. Richard Arnold, Mayor, and some aldermen waited at the City Exchange until the troops were safely across the river then they started toward the Union lines to surrender. They were escorted to General Geary who took the surrender which said:

"I respectfully request your protection of the lives and private property of our citizens and women and children."

General Geary agreed and said that any violation would mean death! Geary led the procession of Union forces into town and raised the Union flag over the City Exchange and made appropriate speeches. But where was General Sherman? It would be the next day until Sherman arrived as he had decided to come up the river in a boat, the *Harvest Moon,* and it got stuck in the mud with him aboard! He stayed the first night at the Pulaski House Hotel and there received callers including the wealthy merchant, Charles Green, who offered his house on Madison Square. Sherman accepted and stayed at the place now referred to as the Green-Meldrim House. It was from there that Sherman sent his famous telegram:

"To his Excellency

Dear Sir: President Lincoln
I beg to present you as a Christmas gift, the City of
Savannah with 150 heavy guns and plenty of
ammunition and also about 25,000 bales of cotton.

W.T.Sherman, Maj.Gen."

That there was any cotton to present, indeed any city to have surrendered, may have been due to a man named Charles Clark Miller.

Green-Meldrim House on Madison Square

Miller was the stock manager of the Central of Georgia Railroad. He had been under standing orders from the railroad to set all cotton in the yards on fire when Sherman approached. Perhaps he recalled the terrible fires that had devastated the city. As Sherman neared the city there was a high wind and he knew if he burned the cotton the city would burn to the ground. He decided to disobey his orders and probably saved the city!

77

Sherman did not burn Savannah but he burned right up to the city and many, many plantations were lost. After the city surrendered, there was a little looting. One soldier went into a store and took a fireman's hat and when General Geary saw it he stripped the man of his rank and warned others. Geary put out patrols all over the city. Generally, the Union forces behaved but there were exceptions. Mrs. Sarah Davenport, widow of the well-known builder Isaiah Davenport, was living on the northeast corner of Barnard and Taylor Streets and was caring for her three grandchildren, the children of Henry Rootes Jackson. Union men were in the square and had come into some of the houses and taken things. Mrs. Davenport became furious and went to the Green house and demanded to see Sherman. He agreed to see her and she said "I am the mother of six sons, three of whom are serving in the Confederate Army..." Sherman interrupted her and said "Madame, if there is any person deserving of protection, you are that person" and he posted a guard at her home to protect her. Sherman also visited Mrs. William Washington Gordon whose husband was a Confederate general. He delivered letters to her from her father and brothers who were distinguished Union officers.

The Union officers had more to do than just keep order in the city. Four years of war had left the city in a filthy and dilapidated condition. It would take two months for the Union men to clean up the city. There were 568 carcasses removed which had been littering the squares and streets. Also, 8300 carts of garbage and 7200 loads of manure were removed. Buildings and trees were whitewashed. Many of the Union soldiers were camped in the squares, building lean-to structures from whatever wood they could find. Others camped at Colonial Park Cemetery where they also had their horses. Some soldiers dug there as rumors persisted that silver and gold treasures had been buried there for safekeeping. The Union men enjoyed sightseeing in Savannah and they wrote home telling that it was the most beautiful place they had ever been. They especially liked Monterey Square and its monument to Count Casimir Pulaski, a great hero of an earlier war.

It was a time of desperate poverty for Savannahians. No one had any money nor did they have any food. In 1864 a man named Julian Allen of New York did something about this. He collected all the rice that anyone in the area had. He took the rice, by boat, to New York and sold it to raise funds. While there he gave speeches urging help for Savannah. Three weeks later he returned with three ships loaded with food and people quickly got in line to get it. With the sugar they acquired, women made sweets to sell to the Union men to get some desperately needed money. These same women would however, turn their backs on the soldiers when they marched down the streets.

For the most part General Geary's order to protect the citizens and the city was obeyed by the troops through January, 1864 when Sherman left. After that, an order was issued to deport the wives and children of Confederate officers in March, 1865. Later that same month, black troops, the Massachusetts 33rd, 54th, and 102nd regiments arrived to oversee the city. These two events outraged the city.

The War was however about over and soon, the Confederate loved ones would return to the city. Reconstruction, under orders from the United States government, was about to begin.

XIV

Forty Acres and a Mule

A fter freedom, most slaves felt they would not be free if they stayed with their former owners so they left and often crowded into the city. Freedom and the new concepts of working were difficult ideas to put in motion. Those whites who might have hired them were themselves without funds and desperate to see how their lives could be rebuilt.

Education was important to the newly freed slaves as they knew it to be the way to a better life. Prior to the War, it was illegal to teach slaves to read and write. To do so risked a $100.00 fine and a whipping of 39 lashes. Despite this, there were early slave schools such as the one operated in a small house by Jane Deveaux from 1836-64. She had been educated in the north and returned to help teach others. The children were careful to not arrive in groups. She had hiding places for them in her house if the authorities would come. She had few books and taught the children their letters and numbers by using nuts with which she could form letters or numbers. The nuts could easily be put into a basket to conceal their real use. Rev. James Simms was another pre-War teacher who was whipped for his efforts. Immediately after the War, many schools opened, particularly in the churches. There was also a school for 450 students on Fahm Street.

The Beach Institute was built and operated by the Freedman's Bureau. It was named for Alfred E. Beach, editor of the *Scientific American* magazine, who donated money to purchase the site at 502 East Harris Street. The school would be operated in conjunction with the American Missionary Association and a home for the teachers, white women from the North, was erected next to the school. Each student was charged $1.00 a month to attend the school and it was strict with much emphasis on religion. This school and another at St. Joseph's Catholic Church survived but many of the smaller ones did not. In 1865 there were 1877 black students in the schools. By 1870, only 672 students were enrolled. Money, much of it from the north and the federal government had dried up. In 1990 the Beach Institute building was restored and opened as an African-American Cultural

Center. In the late 1870's, descendants of Noble Jones purchased two sites for schools for the education of black children. One, named for its location, was the East Broad Street School. The other was the West Broad Street School located in the William Jay mansion built for William Scarbrough. After desegregation closed this school, it was restored and opened as a house museum.

The King-Tisdell Cottage, 514 East Huntingdon Street was moved to its present site in 1981. Its location is in the Beach Institute neighborhood, traditionally a black neighborhood named for the school. King-Tisdell is a center for learning and preserving black history. The

King-Tisdell Cottage

small Victorian cottage, open to the public, was built in 1896 for W.W.Aimer. In 1910 the house was purchased by a black businessman, Eugene King and after his death, his widow, Sarah, married Robert Tisdell, thus the name.

After the War, with the influence of the federal government, great strides in the black community were made. Blacks were elected to the Georgia Senate and held many important community posts. Some of the men obtained employment at the U.S.Custom House. John Deveaux held increasingly responsible positions and was, in 1896 appointed by President William McKinley to be in charge of the Savannah Custom House. At first, men who had learned skills such as carpentry or plaster work as slaves were able to earn a good living. Some years later however, these workers would be excluded from unions which effectively limited their employment opportunities. The gains made in the early days of reconstruction began to erode as the white community regained its strength. The federal government was no longer around to enforce the laws. Soon there were restrictions on voting and special sections of theaters and such were designated "for colored". In 1875, a black newspaper, the *Savannah Tribune* was founded. By 1880, there were nearly 200 social and benevolent clubs and societies.

Sherman's famous Field Order No. 15 was issued at Savannah's Second African Baptist Church on January 16, 1865. It expropriated the coastal islands of South Carolina and Georgia from their former owners and gave them to the newly freed slaves. The process of distributing this land to the freedmen prompted the memorable phrase, "forty acres and a mule". Unfortunately, the order was only in force for nine months. It was nullified by Congress under President Andrew Johnson in September,1865. During its short existence, it served as a rallying point with the freedmen, who above all else wished to purchase land and establish their own communities. To a certain extent, the free market accomplished what Sherman had been unable to do. In the economic chaos of the war's aftermath, prices fell from $5 to $2 per acre for farm land, enabling some of the freedmen to purchase land. Many of the former landowners had been killed in the war, families had moved away, and some land was simply abandoned.

Within Chatham County there are several small villages and communities that grew up during Reconstruction. One of these is Nicholsonboro, located about nine miles south of the city on White Bluff Road. In 1868, a newspaper article reported that the freedmen of St. Catherine's Island had been unable to reach a satisfactory work contract with the proprietors of the island, the Waldburg family. Subsequently, the Freedmen's Bureau of the Savannah District aided the transportation and resettlement of the islanders to the White Bluff area near Savannah.

They first settled at Cedar Grove about a mile from Nicholsonboro, then in 1877, eighteen families purchased 200 acres of land for a total of $5,000.00 or about $4.50 per acre. Their mortgage was paid off in 1882 and an acre of land for a church was set aside in 1883. The settlement seems to have prospered as a fishing and truck gardening community. A small church was replaced by a much larger church in 1890. Unlike many rural churches which have been torn down and replaced or encased in brick or concrete block, Nicholsonboro's two churches are essentially unchanged from the Reconstruction period. They can be seen at 13319 Old Coffee Bluff Road.

The same process was repeated throughout the coastal area as the freedmen moved from the isolation of the islands to the mainland, in search of jobs and education. Churches or congregations that may have originated on the islands are Isle of Hope Baptist and Skidaway Baptist in Sandfly, and Wilmington Baptist on Skidaway Road. Freedmen from Ossabaw are said to have comprised much of the community and congregation of Pinpoint's Sweet Field of Eden Baptist Church and the later church, First Beulah Baptist in Montgomery. Pinpoint has recently become well-known as the childhood home of Supreme Court Justice Clarence Thomas.

Many churches and church missions for the freedmen were established at this time, by all the Protestant denominations, as well as the Catholic Church. After the Civil War, the Savannah Diocese asked the Benedictine Order to establish missions for the education of freedmen. In 1874 a group of Benedictine monks from Pennsylvania built St. Benedicts Church and School on Perry Street. Two years later they constructed a school, chapel and small monastery on Isle of Hope.

Nicholsonboro Baptist Church

The chapel, Our Lady of Good Hope, is located just off Bluff Drive. They established a school for boys on Skidaway Island, which was dedicated in June, 1878 in a colorful ceremony held outside in a nearby oak grove. A school for girls was established by the order of Poor Clares. Of the estimated 80 school aged black children on Skidaway Island at the time, few attended the schools and both were closed by 1889. The last of the monastery buildings, an old plantation house known as Hampton Place, was razed in 1941.

One of the oldest church missions in the Savannah area may have been Ogeechee Mission, established about 15 miles south of the city in what is now the Burroughs community. Originally a church established in 1832 to serve three nearby plantations, it became the Episcopal Church's Ogeechee Mission in 1845. A pastor was assigned, Rev. William C. Williams, and such was his success that his congregation was the largest Episcopal congregation, black or white, in Georgia. After the Civil War, the Women's Auxiliary and members of St. Bartholomew's Church in New York City sent $400 for the construction of new church and school buildings at Burroughs, which were built in 1896. The Episcopal Church supported the school until 1916, when it was incorporated into the public school system. Both the lovely Victorian church, named St. Bartholomew's in honor its donor, and school, now a parish house, can be seen at the intersection of Wild Heron and Chevis Roads.

During this period the Georgia State Industrial College for Colored Youths, as Savannah State College was first named was established. It was the first publicly supported state college for blacks in Georgia. Begun in Athens in 1891, the college was transferred to Thunderbolt in the same year. It was not originally to be in Savannah but local black leaders, including the Rev. James Simms, raised funds and acquired the land so it was established in here. Today the oldest structure on campus is Hill Hall, a large three-story neo-Classical building constructed in 1901 by the staff and students. From the initial eight students, the enrollment has grown to several thousand. Recently, the college celebrated its 100th year of service to the community.

In the early 1900's through World War II, West Broad Street, now renamed Martin Luther King, Jr. Blvd., was a thriving area for black commerce. It is to become the site of the NAACP Civil Rights Museum. During the second World War, Savannah was hostess to thousands of black troops stationed from Parris Island to Fort Stewart. Women from many churches such as Most Pure Heart of Mary, worked unceasingly throughout the war to have dances, plays and parties to entertain the troops. Often these events were in the church social halls or sometimes, in the ballroom on the second floor of the McKelvey Building on Martin Luther King, Jr. Blvd.

By the early 20th century, agriculture began to lose its importance in the Savannah area. Most people made their living in non-farm jobs, either in transportation, such as rail or shipping, or in the industries which had begun to locate along the Savannah River on the old plantation sites. Places along the rivers in the eastern part of the county began to be settled first as vacation retreats called "summer havens", then as suburbs, by people who made a living in the city of Savannah.

XV

On The Salts

On the salts was an expression used in bygone days to describe life on the coastal rivers and creeks. Although resorts, summer havens and other pleasure spots had been present in the Savannah area for many years, the decades after the Civil War saw rapid development of the eastern part of Chatham County due to the train and suburban trolley system. Transportation companies went so far as to build resorts or destinations for vacation and fun seekers, so they would ride the train or trolley. The biggest resort area was, of course, Tybee Island. For years it had been reached by steamers traveling down the river from Savannah. Then in the late 1880's, came the rail line. It was quite an accomplishment, since causeways had to be built through long sections of marsh, and several bridges constructed. When it opened,

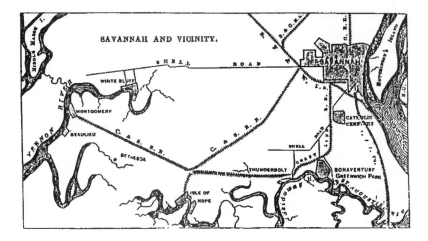

1890 Map of Savannah's Summer Havens

Tybee began to develop at a fast rate, because of the crowds of people coming out on the train! The town of Tybee was subdivided into lots, and incorporated in 1887. Many of the old hotels and boarding houses date from this period, especially at the south end.

The Tybee train continued until the Great Depression, making its final run in 1933 from the station on Randolph Street. The old station building was moved to Fort Jackson where it now serves as a gift shop. By this time the road to Tybee, opened in 1923, had to a great extent replaced the train. Probably the best known of the Tybee pavilions was the Tybrisa, which lasted until it burned on May 17, 1967. It was owned until 1924 by the Central of Georgia Railroad who purchased the Savannah-Tybee rail line from its original builders. Tybrisa was one of several places that had a pier extending out into the ocean with an open air pavilion with a bandstand and restaurant. Many famous entertainers of the day performed there.

Another train system joined Savannah with many of the outlying river and seaside communities or 'summer havens'. In earlier years from about 1840 on, these had been places that the well-to-do had built vacation homes. Now they became accessible to the day trippers and eventually, suburban commuters, who began to use these homes as their primary residences. The suburban train began service in 1871. Eventually it went to Thunderbolt, Isle of Hope, Sandfly, Beaulieu, Montgomery, and White Bluff (Vernonburg). It ran only until 1879 to White Bluff, as the railroad bridge across the Vernon River collapsed that year, and was not rebuilt. In the 1890's a resident of Beaulieu described it as such, "The little train chugged along through the woods in a leisurely manner, with occasional stops to allow the fireman to alight and chop wood for the engine while the passengers got out and picked wild flowers. The engineer also called a halt when he saw a chance to shoot a partridge." In the early 1900's the train was replaced by the quieter but less picturesque electric trolley.

Isle of Hope, Beaulieu, Montgomery, and White Bluff all had pavilions, resort hotels, and tearooms at different times in their existence, but only Thunderbolt seems to have developed into a full blown resort like Tybee Island. By 1895 it had a famous Casino, located where Rivers End Restaurant is now. For many years gambling was legal in Georgia, and was a feature of all the resort hotels! Thunderbolt also boasted of the Yacht Club, located about where Victory Drive crosses Bonaventure Road. The Savannah Jockey Club and a race track were located nearby. Wheelman's Park for bicycles opened in 1893, somewhat west of the town, about where Skidaway Road crosses Victory Drive.

After the turn of the century, Thunderbolt became a center of the fishing industry with the opening of canneries and oyster packing houses. By the 1930's, Thunderbolt's Maggioni's Seafood was one of the largest firms in the area. Perhaps the earliest oyster packing plant in the South was established in the 1880's on the northern end of Wilmington Island. It was begun by Dr. Arminius Oemler, physician and agriculturist, who also published a paper in 1889, "The Life History, Propagation and Protection of the American Oyster". One of the most recent canneries to close was that at Pinpoint, just off Diamond Causeway. It produced oysters and crab until the mid 1980's.

By 1890 a regular ferry operated by the Ambos family was run to Wilmington Island, which had also become a summer haven. Wilmington Island's south end was developed by the "Wilmington Island Pleasure and Improvement Company" during this decade, and later a clubhouse and golf course were built in this area. In 1927 a

Bluff Drive on the Isle of Hope

number of investors built the General Oglethorpe Hotel, an impressive Mediterranean Revival style resort hotel, last known as the Savannah Sheraton. Its golf course was built by one of the leading golf course architects of the day, Donald Ross. The Brotherhood of Railway

Conductors built a retirement home for its members called National Conductors' Home on Oatland Island in the same year. This huge neo-Classical structure is now the Oatland Island Educational Center which supports a small zoo and gives nature programs.

Oatland Island Educational Center

Isle of Hope, Beaulieu, Montgomery and White Bluff saw similar development, only quieter and more residential in character. Isle of Hope's trolley was boarded about where the Isle of Hope Marina is located today, which was the site of one of the pavilions and facilities for boating and bathing. In the early 20th century, one of the Isle of Hope's best known attractions was Barbee's Pavilion and Terrapin Farm. Thousands of turtles were raised here, and the meat exported all over the U.S. They were also a great tourist attraction, particularly for children, who were treated to turtles doing tricks like playing the piano! Mr. Barbee, who must have been an interesting character, took up the turtle business after retiring as a conductor with the suburban trolley.

Residential development was also spurred by the recurring yellow fever epidemics, which seemed to spare the river and seaside communities. Some of the houses in Isle of Hope are still referred to as "yellow fever" houses, because they date from the 1876 epidemic, when Savannah residents fled to this community. Today, the fine and varied collection of 19th century homes on Bluff Drive, together with the ancient live oaks and the views of the river, create one of the most picturesque spots in Savannah. Bluff Drive's charm has been featured in several movies, from "Gator" in the 1970's to "Camilla" in 1992.

Regattas or sailing races were a favorite pastime at Beaulieu, an ideal spot because of its location on Ossabaw Sound. There the pavilion was often used as a gathering place where the spectators came to picnic and view the sailboats. In 1870 the last fatal duel in Savannah is said to have been fought after a dispute broke out between guests at one of the sailing races at Beaulieu. Later, the community became known for its water, which one enterprising resident, D.B. Lester, bottled from an artesian well on his property. It was called "Beaulieu Magnesia", and was much preferred by Savannahians to the heavily chlorinated city water.

The same individual is said to have paid the county $30,000. for the shell road leading to White Bluff, or present day Vernonburg. A toll gate was set up near the present entrance to Ardsley Park on Bull Street, and the fees were as follows: 25 cents for a carriage, 20 cents for buggies, 15 cents for horseback riders, and 10 cents for ox carts. A well-known resort built prior to the Civil War, the Vernon House was located at White Bluff right on the river. It had a large dining hall 60 feet wide in which its famous seafood dinners were served. This resort burned in 1878, and except for occasional tea rooms through the postwar period, the suburb remained essentially residential as it is today.

The International Automobile Races, which were hosted by the city of Savannah in 1908, 1910 and 1911, also served to develop the south side of Savannah. Spectators came from all over Georgia and the U.S. to see the race cars as automobiles were still something of a novelty at the time. The course led up Bull Street to Montgomery Crossroads to Whitfield Avenue to the Shipyard Road intersection. Here the small triangle and road curving to the left are all that is visible of the race track. At least half a dozen of these banked curves were built for the race track, as the racers were to be traveling at the unheard of speeds of 70 to 80 miles an hour. A portion of Ferguson Avenue was built especially for the race. Convict labor was used in the construction and resurfacing of existing roads, but happily for the convicts, they were allowed to watch some of the races from a separate grandstand.

From Ferguson Avenue the course went past Wormsloe into Isle of

Hope on Bluff Drive, then out again to LaRoche Avenue into Thunderbolt. This picturesque stretch of the course no doubt prompted remarks from the race car drivers that they had never driven such a pretty course. The palms were considered especially attractive, and it is thought that some of the palm roadside landscaping was done at this time. From LaRoche Avenue the course ran through several small streets onto Victory Drive. Later versions of the race course in 1910 and 1911 had fewer turns and were simpler. There was also a short course for the smaller automobiles.

Only two years after the races began, the suburbs of Ardsley Park and Chatham Crescent began development. The races served as a wonderful advertisement for the area south of the city, as well as for places actually "on the salts" like Montgomery and Isle of Hope, that the racecourse passed through. More land to the south of Savannah had became available thanks to the Casey Canal project, begun in the 1880's as a health measure to combat yellow fever by draining wetlands. It allowed the reclamation of a large area between Waters Avenue and Skidaway Avenue which had been known as "Cuyler Swamp". Midtown and Southside Savannah developed as small farms, and later dairies, after the boll weevil began to decimate the cotton crop in the early 1920's. Local farmers originally began selling milk to raise cash when the cotton crop failed, but many eventually went full-time into the dairy business. Several modern subdivisions, such as Kensington and Oakhurst, were named for the dairy farms whose land they occupied. Another dairy, Annette's, was located at present Grayson Stadium and Daffin Park.

Because of Savannah's importance as a port, wartime industries such as shipbuilding created a surge of prosperity during and after World Wars I and II. All along the Savannah River these industries contributed to the development of Port Wentworth, Garden City and East Savannah. Even the Spanish-American War saw the development of Fort Screven at the northern end of Tybee Island.

XVI

Only Yesterday

After the Civil War, a nationwide assessment of coastal defenses was made and many defenses were then bolstered. As a part of this effort, in 1872, the U.S. Army Corps of Engineers drew up plans for the construction of a fort on Tybee Island. It was not until 1896 that funds were appropriated and construction of what was initially called Ft. Tybee began. By presidential proclamation the name was changed in 1899 to Ft. Screven to honor General James Screven, Revolutionary War hero, killed in action near Midway, Georgia in 1778.

During the Spanish-American War the defenses at Ft. Screven and other coastal forts were enhanced. The 154' Tybee Lighthouse was used as a communications platform and was key to area defense. The gun batteries constructed around the north end of the island can still be seen. The Tybee Museum is in one of them, Battery Garland. During World War I some of the guns were dismantled and sent to France for use against Germany. Other guns remained at Ft. Screven until 1942 when, considered obsolete, they were melted for reuse in World War II. The Eighth Infantry was stationed at the Fort after their return from Germany in 1923. Then in 1940 the Coastal Artillery Corps took control and at the end of World War II, the Army declared the fort surplus and it was closed in 1945. The town of Tybee Island then purchased the entire area.

The early 1900's was a period of diverse growth in the area. Continuing a tradition that began with the earliest's settlers in Trustee's Garden, the area developed another agricultural experimental station generally referred to as the Bamboo Farm. In the 1890's a Mrs. Smith planted three small bamboo shoots which had been given her by a neighbor, Andrew Moynelo who brought home a single plant from Japan. In 1915 an employee of Mrs. Smith's, Colonel Drayton, sent a sample of the bamboo to the United States Department of Agriculture (USDA) in Washington, D.C. There it came to the attention of Dr.

David Fairchild and Barbour Lathrop. The USDA acquired the property in 1919 and Lathrop donated $10,000. toward the erection of two Japanese style structures which were completed in 1929. The entire complex is 46 acres including a two acre grove of Giant Japanese Timber Bamboo visible from the entrance on Canebrake Road at Route 17. The cut bamboo is often sent to zoos to feed the pandas.

One early 20th century Savannah man remembered at his death, not only his fellow citizens but the animals of the community. In his will Percival R. Cohen left funds for Cohen's Retreat Rest Home for adults, the Fresh Air Home at Tybee Island for the children, and $2500. for the erection of a humane fountain for the hardworking horses that hauled cotton wagons and for dogs. The Percival R. Cohen Fountain was designed by architect Henrik Wallin and erected in 1934 on Bay Street at Whitaker Street. Soon however, the downtown ran out of horses and in the summer of 1945, it was moved to its present location on Victory Drive at Bull Street in the median. The fountain says on the plaque at its base "The Percival R. Cohen Fountain for the comfort of horses and dogs".

Percival R. Cohen Fountain on Victory Drive

In 1940 Savannah's population was 95,996. This population would greatly increase during World War II as the location as a port made the city a hub of activity. Huge quantities of supplies were sent from the city by the War Department, especially bombs, tanks and other weapons. The port particularly supplied the British Army and the RAF. At the end of the war the flow continued as 900,000 tons of rebuilding materials such as steel, lumber, and cotton were shipped. This supply line had to be maintained and made Savannah a possible target of sabotage. The U.S.Coast Guard had Police powers and they patrolled every foot of the waterfront 24 hours a day. Every ship was boarded and checked. Anyone gaining access to the waterfront had to have a "Captain of the Port ID Card".

Savannah also was a great shipbuilding center. Southeastern Shipbuilding Corporation built 93 ships costing $190,000,000. of the Liberty and AV type. Savannah Machine and Foundry Company built 25 minesweepers for the U.S.Navy. This ship building brought people to the city from all over to work and additional housing was needed. The Housing Authority completed seven projects, building 2975 homes during the war. Some of these projects included the Nathanael Greene Villas on Bull at 56th Street and the Francis Bartow Homes, two miles west of Savannah at Jasper Spring. For employees of the Southeastern Shipbuilding, the city built 750 houses on Gwinnett Street in five months, the Josiah Tattnall Homes, and another 150 on President Street, the Moses Rogers Grove. All the structures were designed by architect Cletus W. Bergen.

Camp Stewart, named for Revolutionary War General Daniel Stewart,was established in 1940 as the home base for the 70th Coast Artillery. At its peak during World War II, there were 40,000 people on base. It was a POW Center for German and Italian prisoners. It was renamed Ft. Stewart in 1956 when much farmland was purchased and the base greatly expanded. Hunter Army Airfield was named for Frank O'Driscoll Hunter, U.S. Air Force Major General. He was a member of the Lafayette Escadrille, an ace in World War I, Commander of the Eighth Air Force, and recipient of numerous military honors. The Eighth Air Force originated in Savannah and the city has been the site of many reunions of this group. They are planning a Mighty Eighth Air Force Heritage Center in Savannah with a projected opening in the Spring of 1996.

There were 223 soldiers from Chatham County killed in World War II including Staff Sergeant George K. Gannam who was killed December 7, 1941 at Pearl Harbor. Post 184 of the American Legion is named for him.

By the 1940's the Savannah area was not unlike it is today except for the surge of postwar construction which developed east of Skidaway Road and south of DeRenne Avenue, then mostly a rural area. Savannah had over 200 industries including a cottonseed oil plant, sugar refinery, a paper mill, twelve fertilizer plants, many lumber mills, a cigar factory and a seafood cannery. There were three golf courses and a polo field, nine movie houses, mostly downtown but only one radio station and one theater. Bus fare was eight cents and swimming was allowed in the artificial lake in Daffin Park. The downtown area was no longer the fashionable enclave it had once been and many buildings were deteriorating. Some were even being demolished and this activity would sow the seeds for preservation proponents to act. Happily, a historic Renaissance was about to begin.

XVII

Preservation at Last!

W e are all able to enjoy the beauty and charm that is the Savannah area today because of the many voices, soft and loud, that over the years cried out when historic places were threatened. Preservation is an aesthetically driven movement, often, as here in Savannah, done by women who did not want to loose more of their architectural heritage.

There were many early private efforts to preserve and enhance landmarks. In the 19th century beautification committees worked on enhancing the squares. In 1921 a Society for the Preservation of Parks was formed to stop attempts to destroy the squares. They would wage battles until the 1950's, winning some, others not. There was a Commission for the Preservation of Landmarks formed by the mayor in 1935 that fought demolition threats. There were many private owners who worked to restore properties. In 1945 Hansell Hillyer, then president of the Savannah Gas Company and his wife began to restore the houses around Trustees Garden and the Pirate's House on East Broad Street. This was the first large scale restoration.

In 1951, the Owens-Thomas House was bequeathed to the Telfair Academy of Arts and Sciences and opened as a house museum. In 1953 the Girl Scouts of the U.S.A. purchased the Wayne-Gordon House which they developed into a house museum to preserve the birthplace of their founder, Juliette Gordon Low. In 1954, the old City Market on Ellis Square was torn down amid cries of outrage. The next year when Davenport House was to be leveled for a parking lot, seven women joined together, bought the house and began its restoration. In 1963 the Davenport House opened as a house museum.

Those seven ladies started a movement that in 1955 would become the Historic Savannah Foundation and its charter stated that their goal would be "to acquire, hold, improve, preserve, develop, and restore sites, buildings, residences, and the squares which are a part of the original plan of Savannah and to preserve neighborhood design in mass and scale and proportion, as well as other structures of historical interest in and around Savannah, Chatham County, Georgia, and to increase and diffuse knowledge and greater appreciation of such sites and structures".

Marshall Row, Oglethorpe Avenue

This lofty undertaking would be started by taking an inventory of all buildings in the downtown historic district. This *Historic Savannah Survey* was published in 1967 and listed, dated and rated all structures. One problem was that Savannah gray bricks, made at the Hermitage Plantation, and used for most of the historic houses, had become desirable building material for suburban houses so historic property was being torn down to get the bricks. Demolition had begun on Marshall Row on Oglethorpe Avenue to get the bricks when preservationists put their funds together and quickly bought the property before more damage was done! Realizing that sometimes buying a building was the only way to save it, Historic Savannah Foundation formed a Revolving Fund which became a primary instrument in saving structures. With this fund, endangered buildings could be purchased and held until a buyer who would restore the structure could be found. By 1965 federal funds became available for the rehabilitation of historic properties and this gave a tremendous boost to local activities. Troup Square and Pulaski Square were two areas that underwent major restoration during that period.

In 1966 the area of the original city plan: East Broad Street to West Broad Street, now Martin Luther King, Jr. Blvd., and the Savannah River south to Gaston Street, was designated officially as a NATIONAL HISTORIC LANDMARK DISTRICT. A national treasure! It was not until 1973 that a Historic Zoning Ordinance was enacted by the city and in the interim, some structures were built that might not have been permitted had the ordinance been in place.

The Zoning Ordinance established rules governing exteriors of properties in the Landmark District. The Secretary of the Interior's Standards were adopted for rehabilitation of historic structures. A Historic Review Board was established which continues to rule on all alterations to the exteriors of structures in the Landmark District. Any property owner wishing to change the exterior of his property must submit plans and receive approval from the review panel, composed of private citizens and guided by the City Historic Preservation Office.

Other areas of Chatham County are also of great historical interest. Many individual buildings and several historic districts have been placed on the National Register of Historic Places. After the Civil War, when the trolley lines were extended beyond Forsyth Park, the Victorian District began to be developed. This area, from Anderson Street to the north, Victory Drive to the south, and East Broad Street and Martin Luther King, Jr. Blvd. to the east and west, was placed on the National Register in 1974. Beach Institute Historic Neighborhood, an African American community, was given a designation within the Landmark District itself. The Central of Georgia Railroad Complex was entered on the National Register in two nominations, the Railroad Shops in 1976 and the Train Station in 1978.

Just south of Victory Drive, are the subdivisions of Ardsley Park and Chatham Crescent, both of which began in the early years of the 20th century. Ardsley Park, laid out by William Lattimore, repeated the pattern of buildings surrounding squares. The adjoining area Chatham Crescent, was conceived by Harvey Granger who had developed Route 17, the Coastal Highway. His plan was to build a luxury hotel, now the old Savannah High School, which would attract northern visitors. While staying in his hotel, he planned to sell them a house in the neighborhood. The Depression brought an end to the plan. This area was placed on the National Register in 1985.

Two National Register Districts exist outside the city of Savannah. Ft. Screven Historic District on Tybee Island which includes the historic fort buildings of 1897-1945, was added in 1982. The Isle of Hope, always an area of active preservation, was included two years later.

Individual buildings and historic sites such as Ft. Jackson, archaeological sites such as the Wormsloe Ruins, and plantation homes such as Wild Heron, often entered the National Register as individual sites. These listings, aside from the prestige, offer protection to the area, structure or site as regulations protect the listing from any unauthorized alteration or destruction.

Historic Preservation is an on-going effort that requires constant vigilance as the buildings, squares, forts, monuments, streets and walks require constant care to maintain their historic charm. In 1821 John M. Harney wrote a long poem entitled *A Farewell to Savannah* in which he noted what he saw as the many flaws in the city. At the end of the poem he wrote:

"I leave you Savannah - a curse that is far
the worst of all curses - remain as you are!"

For those people who know and love Savannah, this is not so much a curse as a blessing that the city has been preserved for all to enjoy.

XVIII

And Now . . . Go See It

Savannah has so many wonderful places to visit that a person may not know where to begin exploring the area. These special interest packages have been developed to provide a focus for visiting area sites. In each package, there are only brief descriptions given of the place. If more information is desired, consult the index at the back of this book for the page that will give additional information.

VISITORS CENTER

This facility, located in the old Central of Georgia Passenger Station, is operated by the Chamber of Commerce to provide information about the area. Guided tours of the Landmark Historic District leave from this site. The following can be obtained there:

1. Maps which will be marked with directions to any area destination.
2. Maps outlining self-guided walking or driving tours of the historic district.
3. Tours by trolley, mini-bus, or horse & carriage depart every few minutes from this Center.
4. Audio-visual presentations are available to acquaint visitors with area attractions.
5. Brochures/coupons for area attractions, restaurants, accommodations and shops are here.
6. Books, maps, and brochures about points of interest throughout Georgia may be obtained.

ANNUAL EVENTS

This is but a sampling of the many, many events scheduled throughout the year in the Savannah area.

FIRST SATURDAY on River St.......crafts, music, food!

GEORGIA WEEK......special events scheduled around the time of Georgia's founding, February 12.

ST. PATRICK'S DAY PARADE......March 17th, one of the country's largest parades, lasts 3-4 hours!

ANNUAL SPRING TOUR OF HOMES ......private homes on tour and special events, generally the last week of March.

ARTS ON THE RIVER.......This May event has symphony, ballet, folk music, & arts & crafts along River St.

FOURTH OF JULY......Many events on River St. ending with spectacular fireworks over the Savannah River!

OCTOBERFEST......a party on River St. featuring food, beer, & music with a distinctly German flavor!

CHRISTMAS TOUR OF HOMES......private homes all dressed in their holiday best are on this December tour.

FOR THE CHILDREN

1. SAVANNAH HISTORY MUSEUM, Martin Luther King, Jr.Blvd. at Louisville Rd., has varying exhibits about Savannah history.

2. RAILROAD SHOPS & ROUNDHOUSE, Martin Luther King, Jr. Blvd., next to the museum, displays trains & their repair process.

3. JULIETTE GORDON LOW BIRTHPLACE, Bull St. at Oglethorpe Ave., is operated by the Girl Scouts of America to honor Mrs. Low who founded the organization in Savannah in 1912.

4. FT. JACKSON, President St., near the historic district, and FT. PULASKI, Rt. 80 near Tybee Island, depict the soldier's life in by-gone eras and there is lots of room to run!

5. OATLAND ISLAND, off President St. on Sandtown Rd., is a wildlife habitat and there are trails & educational exhibits.

6. TYBEE ISLAND LIGHTHOUSE, Rt. 80 at Tybee Island, can be climbed. There is also a museum.

7. TYBEE ISLAND is Savannah's ocean beach and nearly all of it public beach. There are high sand dunes with little bridges leading to the ocean.

8. SAVANNAH SCIENCE MUSEUM, 4405 Paulsen St., has varying displays geared to children and hands on exhibits.

9. SKIDAWAY INSTITUTE OF OCEANOGRAPHY, on McWhorter Road on Skidaway Island, features an aquarium and many exhibits about sea life.

AFRICAN - AMERICAN HERITAGE

1. FIRST AFRICAN BAPTIST CHURCH, 23 Montgomery St. at Franklin Square, founded in 1788, the church was built in 1859.
2. FIRST BRYAN BAPTIST CHURCH, 559 W. Bryan St., said to be the oldest parcel of black owned real estate in the country.
3. SECOND AFRICAN BAPTIST CHURCH, 123 Houston St., site of Sherman's order promising "Forty acres & a mule".
4. BEACH INSTITUTE, Price St. at Harris St., established in 1867 to educate the newly freed slaves, it is now a cultural center.
5. KING-TISDELL COTTAGE, 514 Huntingdon St., is an 1896 Victorian cottage, fully restored, now a black history center.
6. LAUREL GROVE -SOUTH CEMETERY, west end of 37th St., contains the graves of early leaders in the black community.
7. ST. BARTHOLOMEW'S CHURCH, Chevis Road., is a Victorian Church, built in 1896, in the Gothic style.
8. NICHOLSONBORO CHURCH, 13319 Old Coffee Bluff Rd., was built in 1890.
9. PINPOINT COMMUNITY, near the Diamond Causeway, childhood home of Supreme Court Justice Clarence Thomas.
10. SAVANNAH STATE COLLEGE, Thunderbolt, was established in 1891.

ARCHAEOLOGY

1. WORMSLOE HISTORIC SITE, Skidaway Rd. at the Isle of Hope, has exhibit of archaeology and tabby ruins.
2. SAVANNAH-OGEECHEE CANAL, Ft.Argyle Rd., old locks and remnants of early commerce.
3. SAVANNAH WILDLIFE REFUGE, Rt. 17 North, remnants of early rice culture.
4. SKIDAWAY STATE PARK, has Indian shell middens, Civil War fortifications, moonshiners stills.
5. SKIDAWAY INSTITUTE OF OCEANOGRAPHY, has exhibits of Indian artifacts.
6. SAVANNAH SCIENCE MUSEUM, 4405 Paulsen St., has exhibit of Indian arrowheads.

CIVIL WAR

1. FT. McALLISTER, south of Savannah at the Richmond Hill exit off I-95, where Sherman ended his March to the Sea. This earthenwork fortification is open to the public.
2. FT. JACKSON, President St., is the oldest standing fort in Georgia.
3. FT. PULASKI, Rt. 80 east at Tybee Island, fell to Union forces after 30 hour bombardment by first use of rifled cannon.
4. SITE at Tybee Island from which Union guns attacked Ft. Pulaski. Command headquarters at Tybee Lighthouse.
5. GREEN - MELDRIM HOUSE, Bull St. at Madison Square, where Gen. Sherman stayed during his occupation of Savannah in 1864. It is open to the public.
6. SECOND AFRICAN BAPTIST CHURCH, Houston St. at Greene Square is the site where Gen. Sherman issued Field Order # 15 promising the newly freedmen "Forty acres & a mule".
7. COLONIAL PARK CEMETERY, Oglethorpe Ave. at Abercorn St., where many Union soldiers camped and passed the time making subtle changes to the old gravestones.

GIRL SCOUTS

1. JULIETTE GORDON LOW BIRTHPLACE, corner Oglethorpe Ave. & Bull St., operated by National Girl Scouts of America and is open to the public for tours and special events.
2. ANDREW LOW HOUSE, 329 Abercorn St. at Lafayette Square, was Juliette Gordon's home after her marriage. It is open to the public for tours.
3. Site of the first Girl Scout meetings, the CARRIAGE HOUSE behind the Andrew Low House, on Drayton St., between Wayne & Charlton Sts., it now belongs to the Girl Scouts of Savannah.
4. Juliette Gordon Low is buried at LAUREL GROVE CEMETERY, just off Martin Luther King, Jr. Blvd. on Anderson St.
5. In Gordonston, a Savannah area developed by and named for the Gordon family, there is a Girl Scout Park on Edgewood Avenue. In 1926 Mrs. Low had the iron gates she made installed here but they were later moved to the Birthplace.

MIDNIGHT IN THE GARDEN OF GOOD & EVIL

1. The MERCER-WILDER HOUSE, 429 Bull St. at Monterey Square is the location where the murder occurred.
2. 16 E. JONES ST. where Joe Odom was living when he met the book's author, John Berendt.
3. CLARY'S RESTAURANT, corner of Abercorn St. and Jones St. is the neighborhood eatery where many of the featured characters met for breakfast.
4. The HAMILTON-TURNER HOUSE on Lafayette Square was the house Joe Odom moved to and opened for tourists. It is now operated by "Mandy" and is open to the public.
5. CLUB ONE on Jefferson St. at Bay St. is the nightclub where the Lady Chablis still frequently performs.
6. BONAVENTURE CEMETERY, off E. Victory Dr. on Bonaventure Rd., where the cover statue was photographed and where the author had cocktails at Conrad Aiken's grave. Voodoo items were acquired here also.

REVOLUTIONARY WAR

1. WASHINGTON GUNS, Bay St. just east of Savannah City Hall, these guns from Yorktown were presented to the city by President Washington after his 1791 visit to the city.
2. BATTLEFIELD PARK, Martin Luther King, Jr. Blvd. at the Visitors Center, was the site of heavy fighting and there is a historic marker detailing the events.
3. NATHANAEL GREENE MONUMENT, Bull St. at Johnson Square, was erected in 1829. Gen. Greene & his son are buried beneath the monument.
4. PULASKI MONUMENT, Bull St. at Monterey Square, was erected to honor Polish Count Casimir Pulaski, the highest ranking foreign officer to die in the Revolution.
5. JASPER MONUMENT, Bull St. at Madison Square, honor Sgt. William Jasper who died in the Battle of Savannah while trying to save the colors.

EUGENIA PRICE NOVELS
Her Savannah Quartet covers 1812-64

1. MARK BROWNING, a fictional character but portrait of Ms. Price's image of him is in the Davenport House parlor. Fictional site of his home was Reynolds Square, across from the Pink House Restaurant.
2. ROBERT MACKAY married ELIZA McQUEEN in 1800 at home of her parents, The Cottage (no longer standing), at Thunderbolt.
3. Their original MACKAY HOUSE, now destroyed, was at 75 E. Broughton St.
4. Mr. & Mrs. MACKAY attended Independent Presbyterian Church, corner of Bull St. at Oglethorpe Ave.
5. Her brother, JOHN McQUEEN, left the Mackays the property at Causton's Bluff on President St. (House no longer there.)
6. The daughter of the Mackays, ELIZA, married W.H. Stiles, a lawyer. Their daughter, MARY COWPER STILES, wed widower Andrew Low and lived in the house now open as a house museum on Lafayette Square.
7. SCARBROUGH HOUSE, 41 Martin Luther King, Jr. Blvd., was the site of William & Julia Scarbrough's "Blowout" parties. The moon & stars were on the ceiling of the entry hall.
8. The Mackay son, JACK MACKAY, attended West Point with Robert E. Lee. Gen. Lee's first assignment out of West Point was working at Ft. Pulaski.
9. The Hampton-Lillibridge House, 507 E. St. Julian St., was bought for the HARRIS-BUNCH families from *Lighthouse*.
10. In Colonial Park Cemetery, corner of Oglethorpe Ave. & Abercorn St., members of the Mackay, McQueen, Smith, Harris, and Bunch families are buried.
11. Other persons mentioned in Ms. Price's books are buried at Laurel Grove Cemetery reached by going south on Martin Luther King, Jr. Blvd. then right, west on Anderson St. into the cemetery gate.

MOVIES FILMED IN SAVANNAH

1. "Forrest Gump". The opening scene shows the feather sailing over all of downtown Savannah. Forrest (Tom Hanks) was filmed sitting on a park bench in CHIPPEWA SQUARE.

2. "Glory" used the MERCER-WILDER HOUSE as the Boston home of the young captain of the Massachusetts 54th (Mathew Broderick) and RIVER STREET, which was transformed into Boston for the victory parade sequence.

3. "Camilla" was in part filmed on BLUFF DRIVE in Isle of Hope.

4. "1969" was also filmed on RIVER STREET between the Drayton and Abercorn ramps where it became Cambridge, Massachusetts. The interior of one of the shops was transformed into a 1960's coffeehouse.

5. "His Name Was Mudd" was filmed in MONTEREY SQUARE, which is frequently used for movies because all of the buildings on the square are 19th century except for one. For the "Mudd" and "Glory" movies the street was filled with tons of sand and dirt to simulate the Civil War era.

6. "Carney" with Jodie Foster used the COASTAL EMPIRE FAIRGROUNDS off Montgomery Street.

7. "Hopscotch" shows the hero (Walter Matthau) renting the summer cottage belonging to his arch-enemy in a house on the east side of WHITEFIELD SQUARE.

8. "Gator" and "The Longest Yard" featuring Burt Reynolds used TYBEE ISLAND for the motel that was blown up, and BLUFF DRIVE and FORSYTH PARK for chase scenes. RIVER STREET was also the place where Burt ran his sports car into river.

INDEX